1st ed

6⁵⁰

BASEBALL'S GREATEST
RECORDS
Streaks and Feats

BOOKS BY HARVEY FROMMER

BASEBALL'S GREATEST RECORDS

Streaks and Feats

HARVEY FROMMER

Atheneum   1983   New York

Library of Congress Cataloging in Publication Data

Frommer, Harvey.
    Baseball's greatest records, streaks, and feats.

    1. Baseball—United States—Records. I. Title.
GV877.F73 1983   796.357'09   82-45939
ISBN 0-689-11385-4

Published simultaneously in Canada by McClelland and Stewart Ltd.
Composition by Westchester Book Composition, Inc.,
Yorktown Heights, New York
Manufactured by Fairfield Graphics, Fairfield, Pennsylvania
First Edition

For my father, MAX FROMMER,
who I hope is on his way to
a great record of his own

ACKNOWLEDGMENTS

Public thanks are extended to: David Szen and the New York Yankees, Bill White, Hank Bauer, Jim Kaat, the St. Louis Cardinals, the Philadelphia Phillies, the Oakland Athletics, the Atlanta Braves, the Detroit Tigers, the Houston Astros, the Minnesota Twins, the Los Angeles Dodgers, Clifford Kachline, historian, and the National Baseball Hall of Fame and Museum at Cooperstown, New York, Marvin Brown, past president of Atheneum, and Larry Sheehan, my editor.

And finally, my sons, Freddy and Ian, for all their aid.

H. F.

INTRODUCTION

Baseball's Greatest Records is a selective sampling of outstanding accomplishments. It is an attempt to both recreate and give perspective to some of the national pastime's magic moments.

"Greatest" is a term that has been and is being overworked. This book has consciously been focused on baseball's truly memorable feats. It is hoped the reader will be able to feel for Lou Gehrig as he pushed himself through the 2,130 games of his heroic streak, and identify with Joe DiMaggio, Rickey Henderson, Lou Brock, Roger Maris, Pete Rose, and Hank Aaron as they assaulted old records and set new ones.

This book eschews the more transitory records created to sell tickets. Thus, Reggie Jackson, poised to hit record home run No. 400, enabled the Yankees and other teams to sell more tickets for a week prior to the event to all those who wanted to be in on history being made. No one reminded those rapping out the press releases that Hank Aaron had 755 career home runs. Additionally, when Pete Rose had one of his hitting streaks going, the press releases and the promos announced: "See Rose hit in thirty-five! See Rose hit in forty! In forty-two! See it in person for yourself and your grandchildren!"

Some "negative stats" have been included here, for they in their own way are as much an accomplishment as the most positive of records, and in a certain way they are more human.

Perhaps all the records, streaks and feats recounted in this book are temporary. Ty Cobb's stolen base record for a season was shattered by Maury Wills, who in turn had his record broken by Lou Brock, who saw his record broken by Rickey Henderson. Roger Maris (despite the asterisk) surpassed Babe Ruth's single-season home run mark; Hank Aaron broke the Babe's career home run record.

As the cliché goes, *records are made to be broken;* they give players marks to aim at and fans things to cheer about. But while we have them, let us celebrate baseball's greatest records, streaks and feats.

H. F.

CONTENTS

HITTING

ix

Contents

PITCHING

Contents

FIELDING

Contents
RUNNING

MANAGING

PHENOMENA

Contents

ENDURANCE

xiii

ILLUSTRATIONS

xv

Illustrations

BASEBALL'S GREATEST
RECORDS
Streaks and Feats

HITTING

Singles, doubles, triples, home runs, sacrifice hits, runs batted in—all are part of what hitting is all about. And so are the streaks, the magic moments, the unexpected rap of bat against ball. This section surveys many of the record achievements, streaks and feats of the greatest hitters of all time, and also includes some special achievements by athletes who had a "once-in-a-lifetime" bit of thunder in their bats. Not described in detail but certainly meriting special mention are the following accomplishments:

Highest Club Batting Average, .3186 (New York Giants, 1930)

Most Home Runs by a Rookie, 36 (Wally Berger, Boston Braves, 1930)

Most Times on Base, 5,282 (Stan Musial, St. Louis Cardinals, 1941–44, 1946–63)

Most Extra Bases in Extra Inning Game, 17 (Mike Schmidt, Philadelphia Phillies, ten innings, April 17, 1976, four home runs and a single)

Most Consecutive Seasons Leading the Majors in Home Runs, 6 (Ralph Kiner, Pittsburgh Pirates, 1947–52)

Most Home Runs in One Month, 18 (Rudy York, Detroit Tigers, August 1937)

Most Seasons Leading Major Leagues in Grounding into Double Plays, 3 (George Scott, Boston Red Sox, 1966, Milwaukee Brewers, 1974–75)

Most Pinch Hits in One Season, 25 (Jose Morales, Montreal Expos, 1976)

Most Strikeouts in a Career, a record still being added to (Reggie Jackson)

ROGER MARIS:
Sixty-one Home Runs in One Season

Roger Maris was an unlikely and unliked hero—the man who broke Babe Ruth's mark of sixty home runs in a single season. "Maybe I wouldn't do it all over again if

I had the chance," he says. "Sometimes I feel it wasn't worth the aggravation."

In 1959, the left-handed-hitting Maris collected thirty-nine home runs for the Kansas City Athletics. The following season he was traded to the New York Yankees. A loner, sometimes surly and moody, Maris thought of himself as the odd man out in Yankee pinstripes.

In 1956, Mickey Mantle had recorded fifty-two home runs for the Bronx Bombers, and there was talk that he was the heir apparent to break the home run mark of sixty set by Babe Ruth. "Yeah," Maris recalled, "they always said he was the one to break the record. He was the favorite. I was never the fair-haired boy over there. When I'd get hurt, they'd think I could still play. When Mantle or Tommy Tresh or someone else got hurt, they'd let them rest."

In June of 1961, Roger Maris had collected twenty-seven home runs—almost half the total that Babe Ruth had recorded when he set the mark at sixty for a season. "My going after the record started off as such a dream," Maris muses. "I was living a fairy tale for a while; I never thought I'd ever get a chance to break such a record."

On July 1, in his seventy-fourth game of the 1961 season, Roger Maris recorded a ninth-inning home run in a game against the Washington Senators. It was his twenty-eighth home run of the season. Ruth's record, all agreed, was reachable.

"Every day and every night," Maris recalled, "people wanted to talk to me—and they all asked the same damn question: 'Do you think you can break Babe Ruth's record?'"

On July 4, in the eighth inning in a game at Yankee Stadium against the Detroit Tigers, Maris slammed a pitch by Frank Lary into the seats. It was his thirty-first home run of the season—and he was more than halfway to the record.

Casey Stengel was asked if he thought Maris had a shot at the Ruth record. "Why shouldn't he break it?" said Stengel, and then, attempting to inject some comic relief into a topic that had turned testy, the wizened pilot added: "That Maris, you know, he's got more power than Staleeen."

Maris, asked over and over again the same question, had grown surly: "How the hell should I know?" was his frequent reply to the frequently asked question.

Maris recalls the atmosphere of the time: "I was a disliked player, and there's a difference when you played as a liked player and a disliked player. I understand why it happened. A lot of people, especially older people, did not want me to break Ruth's record. They tried to make me fit the mold of Babe Ruth, and I didn't want to fit anybody's mold. I'm Roger Maris."

On July 25, in a twi-night doubleheader at Yankee Stadium against the White Sox, Maris slammed two home runs in each game, Nos. 37, 38, 39 and 40. He was two-thirds of the way toward tying the Babe.

The pressure kept building. "I never had a minute to myself," Maris recalled. "People who knew nothing about sports were there in the clubhouse, and they kept asking the same question." Harried, pressured, Maris was called temperamental, moody, miserable. "I might have grown a bit impatient," he explains, "but it never was as bad as they were writing."

Some pointed out that the right field fence in Yankee Stadium was just 296 feet away. Others said too many of Maris' home runs were with the bases empty. Many pleaded openly for Mantle, not Maris, to break Ruth's record. (Mantle would hit fifty-four that season.)

"Every ball park I went into," remembers Maris, "it seemed as if there were 35,000 people there that at least 34,000 would be on my back. It was no fun to hear all those boos. They say it should have been like a duck for me to hear those boos and have it run off my back."

Verbal abuse and fame's relentless spotlight became a way of life for Maris throughout the '61 campaign. Bottles were thrown at him from the stands—even at Yankee Stadium. A game at Detroit was held up as ushers cleared garbage off the field that had been tossed down at Maris. Reporters lined up three and four deep at his cubicle at the stadium. "How does it feel to be hitting so many home runs? Do you ever think of Babe Ruth? Do you get excited hitting those homers? Do you sleep well at night?" Sportswriters and those with just a nodding interest in the game massed about him.

One particularly well-documented exchange is well remembered by Maris. "Roger, you're only hitting .260. Wouldn't you rather hit .300 than bat .260?"

"No comment!"

"C'mon, Roger, answer the question. Maybe you should cut down on your swing and hit less home runs and bat .300?"

"You do what you want and I do what I want!" screamed Maris. "Now get the hell away from me!"

To avoid confrontations such as these, the powerfully built left-hander took to hiding from reporters in the training room. It provided some relief, but the race against Ruth was too big a story. Those who wanted to, needed to, found other places to ask Maris the questions.

Some teams attempted to pitch around him. Maris is still annoyed at being walked five times in one game against the Angels, a game the Yankees won, 2–1, in twelve innings.

"I felt I had to play every day or I'd blow it," notes Maris. "One little injury, and I'd blow it. The pressure from all sides was just tremendous."

Against his former Kansas City team, on August 26, in his 128th game of the 1961 season, Maris recorded home run No. 51. It was just about that time that Commissioner Ford Frick ruled that if Roger Maris broke Babe Ruth's single-season home run record, the feat would be inscribed in the record books with an asterisk to indicate that Ruth had recorded sixty in a 154-game schedule while Maris had played in a season of 162 games.

The Frick ruling angered Yankee fans, who carried placards that announced: "Frick—Up Your Asterisk." Maris was mellower but miffed. "Commissioner Frick makes the rules," he said. "If all I am entitled to will be an asterisk, it will be all right with me. However, I never made up any schedules. Do you know any other record that's been broken since they started playing 162 games that's got an asterisk? I don't. Commissioner Frick should have said that all records made during the new schedule should have an asterisk, but he decided on the asterisk when I had about fifty home runs and it looked like I'd break the record.

"When they say 154 games," Maris later argued, "which 154 games are they talking about—the first 154, the middle 154 or the last 154? If it's the first 154, then the record is still tied. I didn't hit my first home run until the eleventh game in 1961. And if it's the middle or the last 154, I'd have broken the record that way, too."

Despite the asterisk, the pressure of fans and the press, and the interference of some Yankee executives who attempted to encourage manager Ralph Houk to change the lineup to diminish the chances of Ruth's record being broken, Maris pressed on. On August 22, in the sixth inning in a game at Los Angeles, Maris pounded out home run No. 50.

On September 18, the Yankees arrived in Baltimore for a four-game series. Controversy and media hype swirled about. Maris had fifty-eight home runs. His chance to "officially" break Ruth's record was restricted to the first three games—they fell within the 154-game schedule. Accomplishments after that date, the ruling decreed, would be designated by an asterisk.

In a twi-night doubleheader, games 152 and 153, Maris was shut out. On September 20, a night game, his 154th game of the 1961 season, Maris faced Milt Pappas. Reporters had converged on the scene from all over the country. The man they called "Rajah" lined solidly to right field his first time up. In the third inning, Maris caught a Pappas pitch and blasted it almost 400 feet into the bleachers in right field—home run No. 59! Another home run would have enabled him to tie Babe Ruth's record "officially," and two homers would have enabled him to "officially" break the Ruth record in this his 154th game of the 1961 campaign. It was not to be. Maris struck out, flied out and grounded out in his last three at bats that night. "I really gave it all I had," said a frustrated

Maris after the game. "It just wasn't enough."

Number sixty—the shot that tied Ruth's record—was hit in the third inning off pitcher Jack Fisher of Baltimore on September 26. The record-tying homer pounded onto the concrete steps of the sixth row in the third deck at Yankee Stadium. The ball bounced back onto the field and was picked up by Earl Robinson, the Oriole right fielder. He tossed the ball to umpire Ed Hurley, who gave it to Yankee first base coach Wally Moses, who rolled it into the Yankee dugout. The ball and Maris, running out the sixtieth home run, arrived in the dugout of the Bronx Bombers at about the same time. Maris picked up the ball and barely looked at it; cheering fans kept calling for him to come out to take a bow. Finally, Maris emerged and, standing on the top step of the dugout, waved his cap. One of the onlookers to home run No. 60 was Mrs. Claire Ruth, widow of the Babe, who had made a special trip to the stadium to watch the assault on her late husband's record.

The New York Yankees and the Boston Red Sox—the two teams Babe Ruth had played for—met in the final three games of the 1961 season. Amid the trappings of the greatest rivalry in baseball, Roger Maris was questing after baseball's most famous record—home run No. 61, the one that would break Babe Ruth's single-season mark. Red Sox pitchers took the field intent on not surrendering No. 61, the classic number that had stood all by itself for thirty-four seasons.

Don Schwall of Boston stopped Maris in the first game of the series. Bill Monbouquette of the Sox stopped Maris in the second game of the series. On October 1, 1961, in the final game of the season, it was Roger Maris, worn, frustrated, straining, against Tracy Stallard, a twenty-four-year-old Boston right-hander, a rookie.

Stallard retired Maris in his first at bat, and the 23,154 roaring fans at Yankee Stadium were silenced. In the fourth inning, Maris waited in the on-deck circle. In the Yankee bullpen, the pitchers and catchers looked out on the action from their right field vantage point. A $5,000 reward had been offered to the one who caught the ball. "If you catch the ball," Maris had told his Yankee teammates, "don't give it to me. Take the $5,000 reward."

With a 2–0 count on him, the twenty-seven-year-old Maris swung smoothly and powerfully at Stallard's third pitch, a fastball. Sox right fielder Lou Clinton backed against the right field wall, but the ball cleared the wall and pounded into the right field seats as hundreds of fans scrambled and punched away at each other fighting for the ball and the $5,000 reward. "Holy cow," screamed Yankee announcer Phil Rizzuto. "Holy cow!"

Maris trotted out the home run into the record books, the normal tight and taciturn look on his face gone. A youngster jumped out onto the field. He grabbed Maris' hand as the slugger passed first base. Maris shook hands. He also shook hands with Yankee third base coach Frank Crosetti and rounded third heading home. In front of the Yankee dugout, his teammates formed a human wall and would not allow Maris to enter. Four times he attempted to gain refuge in the dugout, and each time he was forced out onto the playing field. Finally, the reticent Maris waved his cap to the jubilant, screaming crowd. The human wall dissolved, and Maris finally was allowed to enter the relative sanctuary of the dugout.

It was the only hit Maris managed that day and the

only run scored in the game as the Yanks nipped Boston, 1 – 0. "If I never hit another home run," said Maris, "this is the one they can never take away from me."

DUSTY RHODES:
Most Pinch-hit Runs Batted In, One World Series

James Lamar Rhodes was born on May 13, 1927, in Mathews, Alabama. A free-swinging, free-spirited type, he was dubbed Dusty and in 1952 joined the New York Giants.

"We used to get a lot of guys like him from up the hill and behind the railroad tracks," recalls former New York City sportswriter Stan Lomax. "Dusty had a lot of idiosyncrasies, but Giant manager Leo Durocher tolerated him. Rhodes produced for Leo, and that was all that mattered. Today in the age of the designated hitter, Dusty would bat .600."

In 1954, the left-handed-hitting Rhodes came to bat 164 times and batted .345. He also managed fifteen home runs and fifty runs scored. It was a season in which Dusty's bat helped power the New York Giants to the National League pennant. However, what Rhodes accomplished during the regular season was just a warm-up for his World Series heroics against the Cleveland Indians.

In the third hour and tenth minute of the first game at the Polo Grounds, with two Giant teammates on first and second, with the score tied, 2–2, in the bottom of the tenth inning, Durocher told Rhodes to grab a bat and "slug the hell out of the ball!"

Rhodes ripped into a Bob Lemon fastball and sent it on a line down toward the 260 mark in right field. Dave Pope, the Cleveland right fielder, scurried back and propped himself against the wall. The ball sailed over Pope's head into the first row of the right field seats. The pinch-hit homer gave the Giants a 5–2 win. It gave Lemon and Pope temper tantrums. Lemon kicked at the pitcher's mound and threw his glove in the air; Pope kicked at the home run ball as it bounded out of the stands and onto the field. "Lippy" Durocher charged over and hugged his good-luck charm, Dusty Rhodes.

Johnny Antonelli of the Giants faced Cleveland's Early Wynn in the second game of the series. In the fifth inning, with the Indians leading, 1–0, Dusty got the call again from Durocher. With runners on first and second base for the Giants, Rhodes stepped into the batter's box. Perhaps remembering too well what had happened to his teammate Bob Lemon, Early Wynn buzzed the ball high and tight to Rhodes, who bailed out of the box and fell to the ground. Wynn's next pitch was slashed into center field by Rhodes for a clean single and his fourth pinch-hit RBI of the series. In the seventh inning, with the Giants leading, 2–1, Rhodes came to bat again and slammed Wynn's pitch onto the right field roof for a home run. It was an insurance run in the 3–1 Giant victory.

The teams moved to Cleveland for the next two games, and some wits remarked that if Rhodes had remained in New York City, the Indians might have had a fighting chance. With the bases loaded in the third inning, Durocher once again screamed: "Go get 'em, Dusty!" Rhodes followed orders. He rapped a single to right field, scoring two runs—his fifth and sixth pinch-hit RBIs of the short series—setting a major league record that has never been equaled.

"Leo liked to keep me around," joked Rhodes, "because he liked the way I dressed up the hotel lobbies." That may have been true, but Durocher's prime reason had to be the clutch-hitting skills of the lanky southpaw whose bat was touched with magic for a few autumn days in 1954.

JIM BOTTOMLEY:
Most Runs Batted In in One Game

In 1924, Jim Bottomley was in the third year of what would be a sixteen-season Hall of Fame career. A powerful left-handed batter, the twenty-four-year-old Bottomley batted .316 that year and drove in 111 runs for the St. Louis Cardinals. And what he did on September 16, 1924, earned him a niche in the record books that few have come close to surpassing. The man they called Sunny Jim drove in a dozen runs in one game.

Bottomley managed six hits off five different Brooklyn pitchers in a game played at Ebbets Field before 8,000 fans. A fourth-inning bases-loaded home run and a sixth-inning two-run homer accounted for half of the Cardinal first baseman's RBIs. Bottomley also lashed three singles and a double. In collecting the record dozen RBIs, Bottomley picked up thirteen total bases.

The ironic part of the record accomplishment was that it broke the previous mark of eleven RBIs in one game set by Wilbert Robinson when he performed in 1892 for the Baltimore Orioles in a game against the St. Louis Cardinals. Robinson, the Brooklyn Robins manager, was an unhappy onlooker as Bottomley shattered one of his records and looked as if he were capable of demolishing another that sixteenth day of September. The other record, seven straight hits in one game, held, though, for Bottomley came to bat only six times.

Since that record performance by Bottomley that capped a 17–3 Cardinal rout of the Robins, only one player has come close to breaking the record. Tony Lazzeri banged in eleven runs on May 24, 1936, for the New York Yankees.

MANNY MOTA:
Most Career Pinch Hits

He was born on February 18, 1938, in Santo Domingo in the Dominican Republic and christened Manuel Rafael Mota. In 1962, he was a rookie infielder-outfielder for the San Francisco Giants and would forever be known by his baseball name Manny Mota. That season saw the trim right-handed batter record his first pinch hit.

In 1963, Mota was traded to the Pittsburgh Pirates, and he played for them until 1968. An all-purpose athlete, Mota played the infield and the outfield for the Pirates and served frequently as a pinch hitter. From 1963 to 1968, he collected forty-two pinch hits.

In 1969, Mota performed for the Los Angeles Dodgers and the Montreal Expos, batting over .300 for each team and adding two more pinch hits to his lifetime total. His ability to come off the bench in crucial situations and deliver prompted opposing players to say that Mota could come out of bed in the middle of the winter and hit a line drive.

In the decade of the 1970s, Mota really moved into his record pinch-hitting groove. His Dodger teammates called him Poppa because of his age and his ability to take care of the team's needs. Time after time, Mota stepped to the plate, a bat in his heavily veined arms, and almost mechanically delivered key pinch hits in clutch situations. "Mota could get wood on a bullet," said Jim Murray of the *Los Angeles Times*. From 1974 to 1979, Mota collected the astounding total of eighty pinch hits. In 1979, on September 2, in a game at Dodger Stadium, Mota came up in the eighth inning and smacked a pinch single to shatter the all-time record of 144 career pinch hits held by Smoky Burgess.

When the 1979 season ended, Mota had amassed a career total of one-hundred-forty-seven pinch hits and had a gold necklace sculpted for him with the number 147 on it.

In 1980, at the age of forty-two, Mota was reactivated by the Dodgers. Delivering three pinch hits in seven key at bats, he helped Los Angeles in a crucial pennant drive.

With the three additional hits, Mota retired the gold neck-lace with the number 147 and replaced it with a new one that sported the number 150. "I don't know how long the record will last," he smiled, "but I'm ready if the Dodgers need me."

In 1982, Mota was once again reactivated. He managed just one at bat and did not get a hit. Those who saw him at the plate against forty-three-year-old Jim Kaat of the St. Louis Cardinals might have thought they were at an Old-Timers' Game.

Mota signed up again as a Los Angeles Dodgers coach in November 1982. And there were many who fully ex-pected to see him in action once again in 1983 if the Dodgers down the stretch got into situations where they needed a confident and reliable pinch hitter.

JOE DIMAGGIO:
Fifty-six-Game Hitting Streak

In 1933, Joe DiMaggio of the San Francisco Seals batted safely in sixty-one straight games to break the Pacific Coast League record that had been set seventeen years before by Jack Ness of Oakland.

On May 15, 1941, the United States was poised on the brink of war; people talked about the photos they saw in newspapers that day depicting London's Westminster Ab-bey and the Houses of Parliament battered by the bombs of the Nazi Luftwaffe.

The Yankees were battered 13–1 that day by the Chicago White Sox. The fans at the stadium, annoyed and angered by the ineptitude of the Bronx Bombers, booed the team at the conclusion of each inning. The brand-new Yankee double-play combo of Phil Rizzuto and Jerry Coleman seemed tentative, tense. Many in the stands moaned that they would never last in the major leagues. Both Rizzuto and Coleman were taken out of the game before its conclusion as the White Sox poured it on. The Yankee loss placed the team under .500, 6½ games behind first-place Cleveland.

More notice was taken of the first-inning "bad throw" by Joe DiMaggio than of his first-inning single. The Yankee Clipper came up with Luke Appling's single to center field, but his throw bounced off the elbow of base runner Bill Knickerbocker and ricocheted into the seats behind third base. DiMaggio's first-inning single drove in Rizzuto from second base for the only Yankee run. Later Joe Dee twice slashed the ball hard off southpaw Edgar Smith to Dario Lodigiani, but the third baseman came up with good plays to deny DiMaggio hits.

On May 24, DiMaggio was hitless in three attempts as he came to bat in the seventh inning in a game against the Red Sox. To that point he had managed at least a hit in each game he had played since that May 15 first-inning single off Edgar Smith. Measuring out a pitch delivered by Earl Johnson, DiMag singled home two runs, enabling the Yankees to defeat the Sox and keeping his streak alive at ten.

On June 1, DiMaggio hit safely in both games of a doubleheader against Cleveland. The streak stood at eighteen. The death of Yankee immortal Lou Gehrig the next day overshadowed the single and the double DiMag racked off Bob Feller to move the streak to nineteen. The all-time New York Yankee record shared by Roger Peck-inpaugh and Earl Coombs was only ten games away, but George Sisler's American League mark of forty-one seemed out of reach.

On June 8, DiMaggio hit safely in both games of a doubleheader against the St. Louis Browns to tie and break his own previous twenty-three-game hitting streak set in 1940. On June 10 the Yankee Clipper had hit in twenty-five consecutive games and the nation had caught the fever.

On June 14, in a highly publicized match-up, Joe Dee faced fireballing Bob Feller. A third-inning single pushed DiMaggio past Babe Ruth's 1921 record of twenty-six games and positioned the twenty-six-year-old outfielder just two games away from the all-time Yankee consec-utive-game hit mark.

A ground ball by DiMag that bounced off the shoulder of shortstop Luke Appling on June 17 was declared a hit by official scorer Dan Daniel. There was some contro-versy about the decision that moved the streak to thirty games—one game more than the all-time Yankee record. However, a nation eager to turn its mind from war news was elated. News programs and songs were interrupted on the radio: *"The streak is alive! The streak is alive!"* announcers shouted.

A very private person, Joseph Paul DiMaggio became the most talked-about athlete in America. On the streets, traffic stopped and fans clustered about him asking for autographs. He was bothered in restaurants. At the ball park, reporters kept asking the same question: "Joe, how many games straight do you think you can hit in?"

Day after day, DiMaggio would step into the batter's box and stub his right toe into the dirt in back of his left heel. It was almost a dance step. His feet were spaced wide apart, with the weight of his frame on his left leg. Erect, almost in a military position, Joe Dee would hold his bat at the end and poise it on his right shoulder—a rifle primed for action. He would look out at the pitcher from deep in the batter's box and assume a stance that almost crowded the plate. Intent, organized, DiMag was ready.

On June 21, the Yankee Clipper singled off Dizzy Trout of the Detroit Tigers. The streak stood at thirty-four—one game more than the 1922 record set by Rogers Hornsby.

Throughout the streak, two of the most involved observers were Joe's brother, Dom, Boston Red Sox center fielder, and Ted Williams, the Yankee Clipper's arch adversary for American League baseball accolades. Their own personal rivalry and that of their respective teams notwithstanding, "Ted really rooted for Joe," recalls Dom DiMaggio. "They were rivals, but they had great admiration for each other. As a great hitter himself, Ted could really appreciate what Joe was accomplishing." Game after game, it was Ted Williams, playing left field for the Red Sox, who would receive information about Joe DiMaggio's streak from the scoreboard operator at Fenway Park. And Williams would yell to Dom, who played in the outfield next to him: "Joe's got another."

On July 1, 1941, Joe DiMaggio tied the forty-three-year-old record of Wee Willie Keeler by hitting safely in both games of a doubleheader against the Red Sox. On

July 2, the Yankees again faced their archrivals the Red Sox, and DiMag was hungering for a hit to reach forty-five consecutive games and a new major league record. Stationed in center field was Dom DiMaggio, whom Joe had invited to dinner for that evening.

Batting for the first time in the game, Joe Dee mashed a Herber Newsome pitch. The long drive was caught by Stan Spence. In his second at bat, DiMaggio poled the ball to center field. Racing at top speed as soon as he heard the crack of his brother's bat against the ball, Dom dramatically snared the ball to rob the Yankee Clipper of an extra base hit.

Glancing at each other from within their rival uniforms, the two brothers, who rarely showed emotion, revealed to all onlookers how they felt at that moment. "It was a great catch," Joe recalled later. "It was one of the best Dom ever made, but at that moment the only thing on my mind was the temptation to withdraw the dinner invitation I had extended to my brother."

In his third turn at bat, with two teammates on base, frustrated twice, DiMag took no chances. He belted the ball into the seats for what would be one of the fifteen home runs he would achieve during the fabulous streak. The homer gave Joe DiMaggio the record—the only player in history to hit in forty-five straight games.

That night the New York Yankee center fielder and the Boston Red Sox center fielder dined on steak and spaghetti. "You know, Joe," Dom said, "I couldn't have gone another inch for that ball you hit that I caught, but I'm glad you have the record."

The streak moved on. A single on July 5 off Phil Marchildon made it forty-six straight. The next day DiMag lashed out six hits in a doubleheader, bringing the streak to forty-eight games.

On July 8, 1941, DiMaggio played in the All-Star Game and had a brief respite from the daily pressure of the consecutive-game hitting streak. Even in that game, his bat had magic in it. He hit safely, but it was, of course, not counted as part of the official record. "That All-Star Game is a special memory," recalls Joe Dee. "I doubled and Dom drove me in with a single." It was the first time the DiMaggio brothers combined in an All-Star Game to produce a run.

The streak moved to mid-July. People stayed up past their normal bedtimes to find out if Joe's streak was still alive. Radio announcers describing to an unbelieving audience how Hitler's armies were moving deeper and deeper into Russia also described how the Yankee Clipper managed to keep the consecutive-game streak going.

On July 16, the Yankees arrived in Cleveland to start a series with the Indians inside the forbidding open spaces of huge Municipal Stadium. Wherever Joe DiMaggio went, crowds cheered him and rivals talked boldly of stopping the streak.

The memory of the challenges, the breaks, that kept the incredible string alive would always be with DiMaggio. In game No. 40, Johnny Babich of Philadelphia announced to the press that he was not going to give the Yankee Clipper anything good to hit, that he would be pitching around DiMag. A Babich pitch way outside the strike zone was swung at by DiMaggio and slammed back through the legs of the Philadelphia pitcher. "Babich looked like he saw a ghost," smiled DiMaggio, savoring the double he was able to record off a pitch that should have been called a ball.

Between games of a doubleheader on June 29 at Washington, DiMag had felt panic. In the first game, his double off Dutch Leonard enabled him to tie George Sisler's record of forty-one straight games. However, the bat that tied the record was stolen between games. "Move over, Sisler, here come DiMag," the crowd screamed throughout that second game, but the Yankee Clipper was hitless in his first three trips to the plate. Just before his fourth at bat he recalled that he had loaned Yankee teammate Tommy Henrich a bat a while back. Joe Dee reclaimed it and used it to lash a solid single as the crowd screamed: "Forty-two! Forty-two! Forty-two!"

The memory of the tenuous moments of the streak was very much with DiMaggio as the Yankees prepared to play Cleveland, managed by Roger Peckinpaugh, who had been the former co-holder of the Yankee batting-streak mark.

A first-inning single on July 16 off Al Milnar's first pitch extended the streak to fifty-six straight games. DiMag also collected a 400-foot double in the eighth inning off Joe Krakauskas.

On the night of July 17, swelled by an advance sale of 40,000 reserved seats, a crowd of 67,468 jammed into Municipal Stadium, the largest night-game attendance to that point in history. Veteran southpaw Al Smith was the Cleveland starter.

Indian third baseman Ken Keltner stationed himself deep, almost back to the edge of the outfield grass, as Joe DiMaggio came to bat for the first time in the game.

It was as if Keltner were daring DiMag to bunt—something he had not done during the entire streak. On a 1–0 pitch, the Yankee Clipper drove the ball past the third base bag. Keltner lunged, leaped, backhanded the ball in foul territory and fired the ball to first base. DiMag was out.

In the fourth inning, DiMaggio walked. A tumultuous din filled Municipal Stadium as Joe Dee came to bat in the seventh inning straining to extend his streak to fifty-seven straight games.

DiMag slammed Smith's pitch to third. Keltner sped at the ball as the Yankee Clipper ran flat out straining to reach first base safely and keep the streak alive. A deft backhanded pickup and a strong throw by Keltner denied DiMaggio again.

In the eighth inning DiMaggio came up with the bases loaded and one out to face Jim Bagby, Jr., a right-handed relief pitcher who had replaced the southpaw Smith. The huge ball park rocked with noise as thousands screamed out encouragement to the stoical Yankee. With the count one ball and one strike, DiMag slammed the ball on the ground to shortstop Lou Boudreau. It came up on a tricky hop. Boudreau gloved it at shoulder level and flipped the ball to Ray Mack at second base for one out, and the pivot throw to first doubled up DiMag. The play ended the inning and the streak.

The Yankees defeated Cleveland that day, 4–3, but in the dressing room after the game there was an atmosphere of silence and defeat. DiMaggio was calm as he smoked a post-game cigarette and answered questions, hitless for the first time in two months.

"I can't say I'm glad it's over," he said. "Of course,

I wanted it to go on as long as I could. Now that the streak's over, I just want to go out there and keep helping to win ball games."

Linked in history with the fifty-six-game hitting streak of Joe DiMaggio is Kenny Keltner. "I'm glad that I was part of it all," says the former Cleveland third baseman. "To me it was just another game and we were losing and I hated to lose, and I didn't realize until it was all over what had happened, but I heard plenty about it after that.

"I made a couple of great plays against the greatest ball player I ever saw. He didn't only hit. He threw and he caught and I don't think I ever saw him make a mistake. Both plays that I made, they were one way or the other—if I didn't catch the ball, it's a base hit for Joe. Unfortunately for him, the ball stuck in the glove and I was able to get it out and straighten up and throw him out by a half a step both times. It wasn't Joe's day. He didn't show any emotion. You couldn't tell whether he was going good or bad—he kept that same face and attitude all the time. There are no hard feelings. Joe and I were and still are good friends. The odd thing about it is that people now don't remember that I had a pretty good record, but the first thing that comes to their mind when they talk to me is Joe DiMaggio."

With the streak ended, Joe DiMaggio began another one. He hit in sixteen straight games to flush out one of the epic examples of hitting consistency in all the years that baseball has been played—hitting safely in seventy-two of seventy-three games.

The Yankee Clipper finished the 1941 season with a .357 batting average. He led the league with 125 RBIs. Half of his thirty home runs were hit during the streak, as were 91 of his 193 hits.

"You can talk all you want," said Ted Williams, "about Hornsby's .424 average and Hack Wilson's 190 RBIs, but when DiMaggio hit in those fifty-six consecutive games, he put a line in the record book. It's the one that will never be changed."

JOE ADCOCK:
Most Total Bases in One Game

The temperature at Ebbets Field in Brooklyn on July 31, 1954, was 95.3, but Joe Adcock's bat was even hotter than that. The Milwaukee first baseman slugged four homers and a double—for a record eighteen total bases in one game—to lead his team to its ninth straight win, a 15–7 rout of the Dodgers.

Adcock's four home runs came off four different Dodger pitchers: Don Newcombe, Erv Palica, Pete Wojey and Johnny Podres. Two of the homers and the double were hit off the first pitch in those at bats; the other home runs came off the second pitch. All of Adcock's circuit clouts were hammered into the lower stands in left center field except for the second home run, which rocked off the facade between the upper and lower stands.

The four home runs—hit as they were off four different pitchers—set one record. Adcock's thirteen extra bases in one game on long hits set another record. His five home runs in two consecutive games (he had had a home run the day before) set still another record.

"I was using a borrowed bat," said the powerful slugger, "for I broke my regular bat the night before. So I borrowed one from Charley White"—a reserve catcher for Milwaukee. "Boy, I could hardly lift the bat. It was the heaviest on the team.... If I played for the Dodgers, I'd hit more than thirty-five homers a year in this park."

The next day the *Milwaukee Journal*'s front page featured a full-color portrait of Joe Adcock in tribute to his siege-gun slugging the day before. The Braves once again pounded the Dodgers, romping to a 14–6 win, but for Adcock, yesterday's hero, it was just another ball game. His contribution was just a double, although Ebbets Field was jammed with fans expecting the lanky slugger to repeat his heroics.

TED WILLIAMS:
The Last .400 Hitter

In his rookie season of 1939, Ted Williams batted .327. In his second year, he batted .344. In 1941, the man who always said he wanted to be remembered as the greatest hitter that ever lived batted .406. It was the last time any major league batter cracked the .400 mark.

"I had a lot of things going for me that year," recalls Williams. "They didn't know whether to pitch me high or to pitch me low. The league was made to order for me then. I knew the pitchers. I was stronger. I had more confidence than ever, and again I had everybody in doubt. I started off hitting right at the beginning of the season and just kept going."

A perfectionist, the man they called the "Splendid Splinter" lived a book on hitting. He leaned into pitches with that bull-whipping, elastic grace. Those pitches that were not strikes he let go by. At one point, he had a string of thirty-six bases on balls in nineteen straight games. He finished the 1941 season with 145 walks— the first of six straight seasons of leading the American League in walks.

A southpaw swinger, "loose as a goose," as some fans called him, Williams stood at the plate swishing his bat about. His eyes were everywhere, sizing up the pitcher, the fielders, the wind, even those who umpired behind home plate. He seemed to be possessed of a nervous twitch, driven to get wood on any ball that was a strike. "Ted Williams," observed Casey Stengel, "looked like the hitter on the cover of an old *Spaulding Guide*, but when they pitched to him everything happened in just the right way. I bet there wasn't more than a dozen times in his life that he was really fooled by a pitch."

In 1941, there probably wasn't a single instance when he was fooled by a pitch.

There were those who said that Williams had super-human vision. Williams did have extraordinary eye-sight—20-10—but his batting excellence was rooted in dedication. "I was a guy," he said, "who practiced until the blisters bled. And then I practiced some more."

The practice made him a disciplined model of consistency, especially during the 1941 season. "At the start of the season," Williams noted, "I had hurt my ankle, but I was about three for nine pinch hitting. Then I started playing regularly and I fell into a real groove."

His peak for the season was .436 in June. Going into the All-Star Game in July, he was still hitting over .400. He hovered about .402 in the last dog days of August and then moved his average to .413 in September. With a week left in the 1941 season, Williams was batting .406 and Boston Red Sox manager Joe Cronin suggested that he sit out the remaining games to protect his average.

"If I'm a .400 hitter," snapped Williams, "I'm a .400 hitter for the entire season, not a part of one. I'll play out the year."

Going into the final weekend of the season, Williams was batting .3995. On Saturday it was cold and raw, and that day's game against the Philadelphia Athletics was rescheduled as part of a Sunday twin bill.

Only 10,000 showed up in the Philadelphia ball park on that damp and dreary Sunday to watch the double-header that had no significance as far as the American League standings was concerned.

Williams came to bat for the first time. "If we let up on you," A's catcher Frankie Hayes confessed, "Connie Mack"—Philadelphia owner-manager—"said he'd run us out of baseball. I wish you all the luck in the world, Ted, but we're not going to give you a damn thing."

Dusting off home plate, umpire Bill McGowan avoided looking at Williams. "To hit .400, a batter has to be loose, Ted. Are you loose?"

Williams was loose. He lashed a drive between first and second his first time up. "I hit a blue darter to right field," Williams recalled, "my second time up. They used to have horns in Philadelphia, and that one hit one of the horns and put a hole in it." In that first game of the doubleheader the Boston Red Sox legend collected four hits in five at bats. He followed that up with two hits in three trips to the plate in the second game. The six hits in eight tries—including his thirty-seventh home run—set his final batting average at .406. The record feat made him the first man to bat over .400 since Bill Terry's .401 season of 1930 with the New York Giants.

The .406 batting average was amplified by an amazing slugging percentage of .735, an on-base percentage of .551. First in walks, first in home runs, first in runs scored, first in home run percentage, Williams struck out just twenty-seven times in 456 at bats. It was in all ways a banner year for the man who was baseball's last .400 hitter.

RON HUNT:
Most Times Hit by a Pitch

Some of the magic records in baseball history have been achieved through luck, others through great skill. The numbers that belong to Ron Hunt are the result of pure determination.

The scrappy infielder began his career in 1963 in the second year of the New York Mets and ended it in 1974 as a member of the St. Louis Cardinals, coming back to the city where he was born in 1941. In between, Hunt managed to get hit by pitches 243 times—a major league career record. Six straight years Hunt also led the National League in getting hit by pitches to set another major league record. Seven times in his career he led the league in the painful category of being battered by pitches—a league record.

Hunt's lifetime batting average was .273, and what he lacked in talent he made up for in determination, as he readily admitted. "My ability wasn't that great, so I decided to make up for it in some other way. I didn't like getting hit by pitches, but I wouldn't give ground."

Concussions, lacerations, bruises, bumps, scratches— all were part of the price Hunt paid for the way he played. Pitches that were strikes were leaned into as Hunt schemed to find a way to get on base. "It always hurt getting hit by a pitch," he said. "I tried not to rub. I found that my best batting style was to crowd the plate, and that's what I did. I always preferred to get hit where I had some meat rather than on the bone. It didn't hurt so much on the meat."

In 1971, Hunt became the darling of the fans of the Montreal Expos as he "gave up his body" for the cause of the Canadian team. He was hit fifty times by pitches, setting a new major league record, shattering the old one set by Hughie Jennings of the Baltimore Orioles in 1896. And there were those who said that Hunt was born too late and would have fit in perfectly with the rough-and-tumble style of the old Baltimore Orioles.

HACK WILSON:
Most Runs Batted In in One Season

In 1926, Joe McCarthy became manager of the Chicago Cubs. The year before, when he had piloted Louisville in the American Association, he had the chance to admire a stubby slugger on Toledo, a farm team of the New York Giants. In the 1925 player draft following the conclusion of the World Series, the Giants failed to protect this individual. McCarthy promptly paid $5,000 of the Wrigleys' money and claimed Hack Wilson. It was one of the greatest baseball bargains of all time.

Dubbed "the million-dollar slugger from the five-and-ten-cent store," Wilson was a folk hero of his time. His trademarks were parallel knuckles on a no-nub bat handle, and a booming voice that responded to the taunts of rival players: "Yowl all you want; I used to be a boilermaker and noise don't bother me one bit."

A short, red-faced, gorilla-shaped man, Wilson was a member of the Cubs from 1926 to 1931. He drove in more runs during his years with the Cubs than any other player in baseball with the exception of Babe Ruth and Lou Gehrig. Referred to as Hackenschmidt, after a famous wrestler of the time, Wilson ripped by day and nipped at night. He was also called "the poor man's Babe Ruth" because of the $40,000 salary he earned in 1931— second only to the Bambino.

The high-water mark for Wilson was 1930. The "Li'l Round Man" blasted fifty-six home runs and drove in 190 runs. Wilson's slugging percentage was an awesome .723. He led the league in walks (105), and strikeouts (84). He scored 146 runs and hit a home run every 9.6 times at bat.

No player in National League history ever hit more home runs in one season than Wilson. The closest anyone came to Hack's fifty-six was Ralph Kiner with fifty-four for the 1949 Pittsburgh Pirates. Wilson's RBI total of 190 in 155 games created a differential of thirty-five— and no player in baseball history ever had that large a spread. Wilson's closest competition for the one-season RBI record of 190 is the 184 runs driven in by Lou Gehrig in 1931.

With four games left in the 1930 season, Joe McCarthy was replaced as manager of the Cubs by Rogers Hornsby. McCarthy's exit symbolized the decline of Wilson.

"Hack loved the bright lights," McCarthy had observed, "but you could forgive Hack his little escapades because he was always ready the next day. Hell, today they make it a big thing when someone knocks in 100 runs. Hack knocked in almost 200 in 1930. And he was loyal. We got along."

Hack didn't get along with Hornsby. The 1930 season was the crest of Wilson's career. He feuded with the austere Hornsby over conditioning routines and curfews. "He's ruining my career," Wilson said of Hornsby.

In 1931, Wilson managed just thirteen homers and sixty-one runs batted in. Traded by the Cubs to the Dodgers in 1932, Wilson played on for three more seasons, increasingly frustrated as his great power waned.

John McGraw said of Wilson: "He is the greatest judge of fly balls I have ever seen since Tris Speaker." Joe McCarthy observed: "I wouldn't trade him for any other outfielder in baseball. He can hit, run and throw." Despite the praise of McGraw, McCarthy and other baseball experts, despite the 190 RBIs and fifty-six homers in one season, Wilson shamefully is not in the Baseball Hall of Fame.

WEE WILLIE KEELER:
Most Singles in One Season

William Henry Keeler played nineteen years in the major leagues and concluded his career with a .345 lifetime batting average—the fourth highest in history. In 1897, the five-foot-five, 145-pound Keeler batted an incredible .432. A reporter asked the tiny man: "Mr. Keeler, how can a man your size hit .432?" Wee Willie's response has become one of the clichés of baseball. "Simple, Mr. Reporter, I keep my eyes clear and I hit 'em where they ain't."

In 1898, the Brooklyn-born outfielder set a mark for hitting that will probably never be topped. Keeler recorded 202 singles in just 128 games—hitting them where the fielders weren't. It was a season in which the left-handed bat magician notched 214 hits. His batting average was .379, but the incredible number of singles saw him record a relatively puny .410 slugging average.

Another amazing part of the record is that Keeler had 564 at bats in 1898 in 128 games. He walked only twenty-eight times. He never struck out. He was up there, in his words, to "hit 'em where they ain't." It was a midpoint in a cycle for Keeler of stroking 200 or more hits for eight straight seasons, 1894–1900. Quite justifiably, Keeler was admitted to the Baseball Hall of Fame in 1939.

TY COBB:
Five Hits or More in Fourteen Games

Tyrus Raymond Cobb performed for twenty-four major league seasons, recording the highest career batting average in history (.367) and the most career hits ever (4,191) and scoring the most runs (2,244). The Lou Brocks and the Pete Roses have come along to erase Cobb's name from the record book in some categories, but it appears unlikely that the Georgia Peach's record of fourteen games in one season in which he was able to rap out five or more hits will ever be approached.

It is interesting to note that in just one of the fourteen games was Cobb able to manage six hits. That was on May 5, 1925, against the St. Louis Browns—the game in which he pounded his largest total of home runs, three, in his record-setting string. It is also interesting to observe that despite Cobb's stroking of five or more hits in fourteen games, never once did he hit for the cycle (single, double, triple, home run).

All of Cobb's five-plus days took place when he was a member of the Detroit Tigers except for his final one. On August 25, 1927, in the next-to-last year of his fabled career, the man from Narrows, Georgia, performed the five-hit trick as a member of the Philadelphia Athletics— the team he had first recorded five hits against in 1908 in his fourth year as a major league player.

The only players in double figures with five or more hits in their careers were Ed Delahanty, eleven, Cap Anson, ten. Wee Willie Keeler was able to accomplish the feat nine times and Stan Musial and Roberto Clemente each did it eight times.

HANK AARON:
Most Career Home Runs

He joined the Milwaukee Braves in 1954 and ended his career as a major league ball player in 1976 as a member of the Milwaukee Brewers. And when Hank Aaron finally hung up his spikes, he had established records for playing in the most games in a career (3,298), most at bats lifetime (12,364), most plate appearances (13,940), most years 100 or more runs scored (fifteen), most years leading the league in total bases (eight), most total bases (6,856), most runs batted in (2,297), most years 150 or more games (fourteen), most consecutive years twenty or more home runs (twenty), most extra base hits (3,085)... but the record of records is most career home runs: 755! It was the one that made the Babe move over.

"Five or six years before Henry was born," recalls his father, Herbert Aaron, Sr., "I saw Babe Ruth play an exhibition game with the New York Yankees in Mobile. I climbed a pine tree outside the ball park to see him. They tell a story about the home run he hit that day that went over the fence into a freight car on a train that was going by. They found the ball later in New Orleans."

The memory of the Babe's homer stayed with Hank Aaron's father through the years of Hank's growing up, through the times when the elder Aaron managed a baseball team known as Aaron's Whippets. The young Aaron was trained by his father to hit bottle caps with a broomstick to develop his batting eye.

"We'd mark lines in the street," the elder Aaron said. "And when Henry hit that soda cap right, you couldn't find it. Then he got on the Whippets team. He was just fourteen. The others were grown men, twenty, twenty-five years old. He just developed his skill with a real baseball instead of a bottle cap. He made it for himself. He made his bat talk. He learned to watch the pitchers as carefully as the umpire does. He learned to be cool. He learned not to just step up there and swing, but to be a hitter who was ready and prepared."

In June of 1952, scout Billy Southworth filed this report on the eighteen-year-old Aaron:

"...A line drive hitter, although he has hit a couple of balls out of the park for home runs. He has good hands, also quick hands, gets ball away fast and accurately. He gets good jump on ball and can range far to left or right. I like his chances of becoming a major league ball player."

After batting .336 in 1952 at Eau Claire in the Northern League and recording a .362 average with twenty-two home runs at Jacksonville in the South Atlantic League in 1953, Aaron joined the Braves in 1954. When outfielder Bobby Thomson broke his ankle in spring training, Aaron was given his chance. On April 23, 1954, in his seventh major league game, Aaron slammed the first major league home run of his career. It came in the fourth inning off pitcher Vic Raschi in a game at Busch Stadium in St. Louis. In his list of "most memorable homers" exclusive of the ones that tied and broke Babe Ruth's record, the home run hit off Vic Raschi is ranked by Aaron in fourth place.

Ranked first on Aaron's list is the home run he recorded on September 23, 1957. The Milwaukee Braves needed one more win to clinch the National League pennant. With the score 2–2 in the bottom of the eleventh inning, Aaron came to bat.

His Milwaukee teammate Johnny Logan was on base as Aaron faced Cardinal relief pitcher Billy Muffet. The man they were calling "the Hammer" hammered Muffet's pitch over the center field fence. Milwaukee had its pennant. "To that point in time," Aaron says, "that was the most important and satisfying home run of my life." Just about a month before he had collected home run No. 100 against Don Gross of the Cincinnati Reds.

The night after his home run had given the Braves the 1957 pennant, Aaron recorded his forty-fourth home run of the season. It was a bases-loaded shot off Sam Jones of the Cardinals, and it gave the young slugger his first home run crown. That home run is ranked in ninth place on Aaron's personal best list.

Aaron concluded the 1959 season with 179 career homers. Three that he notched in one game on June 21 that season rank in seventh place on his list. "Gordon Jones, a right-hander, was the pitcher when I hit my third that day," recalls Aaron. "It was in the seventh inning. I hit the other two off Johnny Antonelli (first inning) and Stu Miller (sixth inning). That was in Seals Stadium, a great park for a right-handed hitter. The Giants moved into Candlestick Park the next year. It was the only time in my career that I hit three home runs in one game and that was what made the accomplishment one of my personal highs."

Despite his skills, the Mobile-born slugger was not a household name. Mild-mannered, a member of the Braves of Milwaukee and then the Braves of Atlanta, away from the glittering big-city media spotlight, Aaron rolled on, but commercial endorsements by and large went to others, and press clippings, in the view of C. C. Johnson Spink, *Sporting News* editor, "were sparse in relation to Hank Aaron's status as a premier hitter."

On July 3, 1960, Aaron belted home run No. 200 of his career. "Throwing a fastball by Henry Aaron," one shell-shocked pitcher remarked, "is like trying to sneak the sun past a rooster."

Jay Hook of the New York Mets must have felt that way on June 6, 1962, as Aaron cracked his 267th career home run—a blast that he ranks tenth on his personal best list. The home run landed in the bleachers at the Polo Grounds to the left of the clubhouse—470 feet from home plate. Only three other players ever hit a home run into the center field bleachers at the Polo Grounds. Ironically, just the night before, Lou Brock, a rookie on the

Chicago Cubs, had accomplished the feat. Joe Adcock once did it when he played for the Braves in 1953. And Babe Ruth hit shots into the bleachers when the Yankees used to play in the Polo Grounds in the 1920s. In 1923, the bleachers were moved back even farther, and no hitter reached them until Adcock. The long-distance home run hammered by Aaron was made even more special since it was his second grand slam homer in succession. Three days before he had homered with the bases full against the Pittsburgh Pirates.

"Every time I hit a home run it's a thrill, because it's a personal high," Aaron remarked. "I've never been a dumb hitter. It's confidence in what I'm doing. I'm either going to scare the pitcher to death by not hitting the ball, or hit it. I just feel I can get a hit when I come up there. I take pride in doing what I am doing every day."

On April 20, 1966, in the ninth inning in a game played at Philadelphia, Aaron homered off Bo Belinsky. The home run, just eight days into the final season of the Braves in Milwaukee, was the 400th of his career. "It's in eighth place on my own list. It's funny, I didn't find out it was my 400th until after the game was over."

Aaron's home run No. 398 has special sentimental significance and ranks sixth on his list. It was hit on September 2, 1965, off Ray Culp of the Phillies. It was Aaron's last home run in Milwaukee's County Stadium, which the team abandoned two days later.

The move of the Braves to Atlanta in 1966 was a fortunate one for Aaron. The short left field fence in the Southern park was a perfect situation for a right-handed slugger like him. "I really did not go for home runs on every pitch," he notes, "even though people might say that I did. With Eddie Mathews retiring from baseball, I felt I had a responsibility to the club. I had no intention of breaking Babe Ruth's record then; I just took it upon myself to drive in runs and I found that I could hit the home runs and still have a respectable average."

Just how favorable the move of the Braves to Atlanta was to Aaron is revealed in what he called "the hottest home run streak I ever had, so good that I rank it fifth on my personal list." On June 21, 1966, he slammed his twenty-fourth home run of the season to tie the record for the most home runs hit by June 30. It was hit off Larry Jackson of Philadelphia and was Aaron's 422nd career blast.

Aaron batted just .279 that 1966 season—his lowest average to that point in his career—but he blasted forty-four home runs and notched 127 RBIs to lead the majors in both categories. At year's end, his career total of homers stood at 442.

On a Sunday afternoon at Atlanta Stadium, July 14, 1968, before 34,826, Henry Louis Aaron, who was born on February 5, 1934, when Babe Ruth was thirty-nine years old, slugged the 500th home run of his career. The three-run shot off Mike McCormick of the San Francisco Giants smashed against the Fan-o-Gram in left center field. As Aaron trotted around the bases the fans rose to applaud his accomplishment. He became only the eighth man in history to record 500 home runs.

"That was my biggest home run up to then," Aaron said after the game. "And the fans here are so nice to me. I've never had an ovation like that. I can't remember one like that. I'm glad I hit it off a good pitcher like Mike. Somehow it means a little more when you hit it off a Cy Young winner. I'm also glad I hit it good. It wasn't a cheap home run," he said about the blast he ranks second on his personal list. "The most disappointing thing is that my father was here for three days and he just left this morning."

Just thirty-four years old, in his fifteenth major league season, Aaron observed: "After I hit No. 500, I thought I could get 600 easy...714 seemed out of reach."

On April 25, 1971, rolling relentlessly on, Aaron had 599 home runs and was all tooled up for No. 600. The Braves faced the San Francisco Giants and Gaylord Perry at Atlanta Stadium on April 27. "If Aaron gets it off me," said the veteran right-hander before the game, "he's going to earn it."

Number 600 came off a Perry fastball in the third inning with one Atlanta teammate on base. Exultant in the clubhouse after the game, Aaron told reporters: "I said all along I'd probably hit it off a pitcher I know. I guessed fastball this time and got it. I knew it was gone as soon as I hit it."

Pressed by the media about Babe Ruth's record of 714 career home runs, Aaron was evasive. "That's a long way off," he smiled. "I'll just try to get one home run at a time."

Though Aaron did not care at that point in his career to speculate about breaking the Babe's record, the statistics spoke for him. His 600th career home run moved him within 114 of Ruth. When the 1971 season ended, he had smashed forty-seven for the year—his highest season total ever—and was just seventy-five away from the record. And he was still very much in his prime: he batted .327 for the year and drove in 118 runs in addition to forty-seven homers.

On July 25, 1972, Aaron engaged in what he termed his third favorite home run moment. It took place in the first All-Star Game ever played in the Deep South. Introduced to the hometown folks at Atlanta's County Stadium, the durable slugger received a standing ovation from the 53,107 in attendance. Hank responded with a two-run homer off Gaylord Perry to give the National League a 2–1 lead. He received another standing ovation when he was greeted at home plate by his teammates—and the game was interrupted again with cheers for Aaron when he was taken out of the game an inning later. "Coming as it did in Atlanta in an All-Star Game," noted Aaron, "it was just a sentimental thrill."

On June 10, 1972, Aaron slugged home run No. 649 and passed Willie Mays forever on the all-time list. With that home run, Aaron was second behind the Babe—and now talking as he went down the home stretch of the "chase."

"Yes, I think about the record," he told reporters. "I think now I can make it if I stay healthy and if I have a strong man batting behind me so that they won't pitch around me."

Like Roger Maris, who also assaulted and broke one of Babe Ruth's magic records, Hank Aaron's accomplishment was bittersweet: "It should have been a lot of fun," he said. "It should have been an enjoyable time, but everywhere I went people were talking about home runs. The lack of privacy was the main thing. It was a fishbowl. I couldn't go anyplace. There was nowhere I could hide. It lasted two and a half years, I'd say. It was hard to eat all my meals in my room. After the games it was tough. I would have to go out the back way of the ball park."

The closer Aaron moved to Ruth's record, the more glaring became fame's spotlight. "I must have given thousands and thousands of autographs," he said. There were autographs for teammates, for opposing players, for elevator operators, for cab drivers, the children of friends and relatives and strangers. Daily there was posing and primping for photographs with all types of assorted humanity.

From 1973 on, when it seemed apparent that the invincible record of the Babe was going to be broken, all types of mail were generated. Some of the letters were highly positive, rooting Aaron on, hero-worshiping him. Some of the letters were of the "hate mail" variety. They attacked Aaron as a black man going against a white legend's sacred record. "Some of it was pretty filthy," notes Aaron. "After a while, I didn't even read the letters."

The extraordinary precaution of an extra room was implemented on the road in the hotels the Braves stayed at. One hotel room was registered in the name of Hank Aaron but not used. Another hotel room, where Aaron actually stayed, was unregistered and policed by security personnel. "It was things like this," Aaron recalled, "that made the whole thing something of a nightmare."

In 1973, the Atlanta slugger began his twentieth season as a major leaguer. He was thirty-nine years old. He played in just three-quarters of the Braves' games. He managed a home run every ten at bats. At season's end,

Aaron had recorded forty for the year—the oldest major leaguer to match or better his age in home runs. He needed one to tie and two to break the magic number of 714 set by Babe Ruth.

Over the winter, Aaron had a lot of time to think about the Babe and the record. "He'll still be the best, even if I pass him," said the modest home run hitter. "Even if I am lucky enough to hit 715 home runs, Babe Ruth will still be regarded as the greatest home run hitter that ever lived."

The 1974 season opened amid much controversy. The owner of the Braves suggested that Aaron sit out the team's opening games in Cincinnati so that the hometown fans in Atlanta would be witnesses to baseball history. Commissioner Bowie Kuhn balked at the idea. He claimed it would deprive Cincinnati fans of a historic moment. He made it a matter of public record that Aaron was obliged to play in Cincinnati.

"I can remember waking up that day," Aaron recalled April 4, 1974, "and driving out to the ball park with a friend of mine who works for the FBI. We went into the ball park and I had to sit through two press conferences. There was absolutely no place for me to stand to take batting practice. So I just decided I would stand in the outfield until the game got started. . . ."

With two men on base, Aaron came to bat in the first inning against pitcher Jack Billingham. On his first swing of the 1974 season, he smashed No. 714. And the thirty-nine-year-old record of the Babe was tied.

The 400-foot, three-run homer went over the fence in left center field at Riverfront Stadium. The historic home run on Aaron's first swing of the 1974 season silenced for a moment the SRO crowd of 52,154—the largest opening-day attendance in Cincinnati history.

The number 714 lit up on the huge scoreboard in center field above the upper deck as Aaron, elbows back, head up, trotted purposefully, unemotionally, around the bases and the crowd cheered. His 714th home run took place on his 11,289th major league at bat. Ruth had needed 8,399 to record No. 714.

Vice-President Ford and Commissioner Kuhn exited from their red-white-and-blue-draped box and hurried out onto the field as the game was halted. Aaron, under control, loped over to them and shook hands. The tributes of Kuhn and Ford and the standing ovations and the congratulations by teammates and members of the Reds lasted for about six minutes. Finally, Aaron disappeared into the dugout seeking some solitude. The cheering stopped and the game finally continued.

Aaron batted two more times but was hitless as the Reds defeated the Braves, 7–6, in the game played in picture-perfect 63-degree sunny weather.

"Move over, Babe—here comes Bad Henry," proclaimed one banner. That seemed to epitomize the moment.

On April 8, at Atlanta Stadium, before a crowd of more than 53,000 and a national television audience, Hank Aaron girded himself for the moment. "I know there will be some who will be disappointed," he said, "when I break the record, but I expect someone will come along and top me some day."

A razzle-dazzle atmosphere replete with a huge color map of the United States painted across the outfield grass that depicted Aaron's life provided the backdrop. "All the dignitaries were there," Aaron said, "Governor Carter, Sammy Davis, Jr., and all the other entertainers. And they were there for one reason—to see me hit it. You know, there was history that was going to be made."

Commissioner Bowie Kuhn was not there. It was reported that he had a previous commitment. Aaron's father and mother were seated in a private box near the Atlanta dugout. "I knew Henry wouldn't break the record until he got to Atlanta," said his mother, who had not accompanied her husband to Cincinnati to watch Bad Henry. "I knew he would break it in Atlanta so I could see it." In New York City, the widow of Babe Ruth sat in her Riverside Drive apartment. It was reported that she did not have her television set on, for she was too exhausted from an afternoon of shopping with her daughter.

Pearl Bailey sang the national anthem. In the sky there were fireworks and balloons, and the Jonesboro High School Band marched and the Atlanta Boys Choir (which also included girls) sang.

Aaron was given five standing ovations by the huge crowd. Al Downing, the thirty-two-year-old starting pitcher for the opposition Los Angeles Dodgers, who wore the same number, 44, on his uniform as did Aaron, was greeted with catcalls and boos.

Aaron was not even able to swing at any of Downing's pitches in his first at bat. He took a ball, a called strike, and then three more balls and sauntered down to first base as the crowd hooted Downing for walking him.

"Well, Downing just pitched around me," said Aaron later. "The Dodgers were leading at the time and he was behind in the count. He was having some control problems because of all of the commotion."

In inning four, Aaron had his second chance. Downing's first pitch was a ball, inside. Before the game the Dodger left-hander had said: "I'm not going to change my way of pitching to him. I've had good luck with Aaron."

Downing's next pitch was a low inside fastball. "I'm sure he was trying to get it away from me," Aaron recalled. "He was throwing me a lot of screwballs, but he got the ball more to the inside of the plate than he wanted."

In the rain at Atlanta amid the carnival atmosphere and the multicolored umbrellas in the stands, Aaron took his first swing of the night—and the ball rose streaking towards left center field. It dropped over the fence and Henry Louis Aaron stood alone in history with No. 715.

The home run trot was deliberate, calm, as Atlanta Stadium erupted in a blaze of skyrockets and flashing scoreboard lights. Aaron trotted out the home run he had relentlessly pursued, his head slightly bowed, elbows turned out a bit from his body. Home plate was a mob scene of Atlanta players waiting to congratulate him.

Leaping out of the special box seat near the Braves' dugout, Herbert Aaron, Sr., rushed toward his son—perhaps the memory of that long-ago home run hit by Babe Ruth in Mobile crossed his mind—as he embraced the man who had broken the immortal record.

The precise moment was 9:07 P.M., April 8, 1974. "I just thank God," said Aaron, "that it's all over with."

The man they called Bad Henry would play on through the 1974 season and go back to Milwaukee where he had begun and perform part-time with the Brewers in 1975 and 1976. He would complete his twenty-three-year career with a grand total of 755 home runs—more than any other player in the history of the game—but the magic moment of the misty April night in Atlanta in 1974, when he recorded No. 715 that gave him in his phrase "the Cadillac of baseball records," would forever keep him in the limelight and invite comparisons with the New York Yankee legend.

ROGERS HORNSBY:
Highest Batting Average in One Season Since 1900

Rogers Hornsby joined the St. Louis Cardinals in 1915. He had been obtained for $400 from the Denison team in the Western Association. Manager Miller Huggins was dismayed at the right-handed batter's stance—deep in the batter's box, hands at the very bottom of the bat.

Efforts to change Hornsby's stance were not successful, and Huggins snapped: "Well, what do you expect when you pay only $400 for a player?"

Whatever was expected, Hornsby far exceeded. He went on to play twenty-three major league seasons and post a .358 lifetime batting average, second only to Ty Cobb. Three times he batted .400; only two other players in history duplicated that feat: Ty Cobb and Jesse Burkett. And in 1921 Hornsby came within .003 of his fourth .400 season.

Born in Winters, Texas, in 1896, Hornsby had a wintry personality. His nickname was Rajah. It was both a mocking pronunciation of his first name and a reference to his petulant personality. Yet, it mattered little to him what others thought. He lived to display what he knew was a regal talent.

"Rogers was all baseball during the game," recalled his former teammate pitcher Pop Haines. "If you gave all you had when you played with him, he was happy. But if you didn't, he'd give you hell. Rogers was a loner, though. He never palled around with any of the other players."

A loner, a nonsmoker, nondrinker, Hornsby never went to the movies or read a newspaper. He was determined to "save his eyes" for baseball. All baseball, he even neglected to attend his mother's funeral when she died on the eve of a St. Louis Cardinal World Series.

Sportsman's Park, the home of the Cardinals, was tailor-made for him. From his position deep in the batter's box, his striding swing took him directly into the ball, and he pulled when he needed to or lashed the ball to the power alley that ran 354 feet in right center field. Once he made contact with his bat, he moved quickly to first base. There were those who ranked him at the very top of the class among right-handed batters in getting down the line to first.

Seven times Hornsby won National League batting titles—six of those crowns in a row. In 1924, Hornsby recorded his crown-jewel season. The Rajah batted .424— the highest batting average achieved by a major leaguer in the twentieth century. He had batted .401 two years before and a year later would bat .403, but 1924 was Hornsby's high-water mark.

It was a year in which he led the league in hits (227),

doubles (forty-three), slugging percentage (.696), walks (eighty-nine), total bases (373). He struck out a mere thirty-two times in 536 at bats.

Experts bicker over who was the greatest hitter of all time, and Hornsby's name always comes into the discussions. If he wasn't the best that ever lived, there is little doubt that he was the top right-handed hitter and the best that ever performed in the National League.

BABE RUTH:
The Greatest Slugger

Hank Aaron eclipsed Babe Ruth's career home run mark of 714; Roger Maris (asterisk notwithstanding) broke the Babe's single-season home run mark of sixty, but the man they called the Sultan of Swat and the Colossus of Clout still ranks as the greatest slugger of all time.

Twelve times Ruth won the home run title. Four times he hammered fifty or more home runs in a season, and eleven times he recorded forty or more home runs in a season; no one else ever came close to these marks. In 1927–28, he lashed a total of 114 home runs, another major league record. Ruth hit two or more home runs in a game seventy-two times in his career—another all-time record. And his career home run ratio (a home run for every 100 at bats) is 8.5, the highest in history. Aaron's home run ratio by comparison was 6.1.

"I could have hit a lifetime .600 average," said the Babe, "but I would have had to hit them singles. The people were paying to see me hit home runs—and anyway, singles hitters don't drive Cadillacs."

In 1920, the southpaw swinger lashed fifty-four home runs, thirty-six doubles, and nine triples and wound up with the astonishing slugging percentage (the ratio of total bases achieved to number of times at bat) of .847. No other player had ever cracked the .800 slugging barrier. The Babe did it twice. In 1921, Ruth finished with an .846 slugging mark. He also holds the third highest season slugging mark, .772, recorded in 1927—the year he hit sixty home runs.

The 1920 season was the six-foot-two, 215-pound slugger's first as a New York Yankee, and he was intent on showing the baseball world his awesome power. His incredible .847 slugging percentage was beefed up by his record home run pace—a round tripper every 11.8 times to the plate, another all-time record. Ninety-nine of Ruth's 172 hits in that 1920 season were extra base hits. And the .847 slugging percentage was helped along by the Bambino's league-leading walks—148, an average of more than one per game. He was on base 379 times in 1920—another all-time record.

Twelve times Ruth led the major leagues in slugging percentage—seven of those years in a row, other all-time records. His .690 lifetime slugging percentage is the highest in history. Ted Williams at .634 and Lou Gehrig at .632 are a distant second and third. Only three times in his career did Ruth slip below the .600 slugging mark in a season.

Other statistics revealing why Ruth was the greatest

slugger include: most consecutive seasons with a .600 + slugging percentage (seven); most seasons with an .800 + slugging average (two); most seasons with a .700 + slugging percentage (nine); most seasons with a .700 + slugging average (three).

Baseball's greatest slugger had Yankee Stadium nicknamed for him, "the House That Ruth Built." The right field stands at the stadium were called "Ruthville," and his tape-measure home runs were dubbed "Ruthian clouts."

There were very few cheap shots among his 714 career home runs. And there were quite a few that were of epic proportions. At Navin Field in Detroit in June of 1926, Ruth homered over the low right field wall. The ball slammed off the roof of a parked automobile and was found two blocks away on Plum Street. It was estimated that Ruth had hammered the ball 602 feet and that it rolled another 200 feet off the roof of the car.

In May of 1935 as a member of the Boston Braves, in a game at Pittsburgh, Ruth hit the last three home runs of his career. Home run No. 714, his last hurrah, was tagged an estimated 600 feet. It was the first time anyone had cleared the right field roof at Forbes Field with a home run.

George Herman Ruth was called Monk or Monkey by some of his opponents, Jidge by most of his teammates, the Sultan of Swat by sportswriters. Fans knew him as the Bambino and the Babe. Perhaps the label that is most appropriate is Babe Ruth: baseball's greatest slugger.

TY COBB:
Highest Career Batting Average

Tyrus Raymond Cobb was many things to many people: a great base stealer, a one-man baseball team, a too-nasty competitor. Many of his records have been surpassed by the Hank Aarons and the Lou Brocks and the Pete Roses, but his lifetime batting average of .367 is a mark that seems to be fated to be one of baseball's most enduring records.

For twenty-three straight seasons, the Georgia Peach batted .300 or more. In 1911, he batted .420, and the following season, he hit .410. Those back-to-back seasons did much to help pad his lifetime .367 average. In 1924, when he was thirty-seven years old, Cobb batted .401. And in his final major league season (he was forty-two years old), the man from Narrows, Georgia, still had enough left to hit the ball at a .323 clip.

They still marvel at Cobb's skills today and speculate at what he would be able to hit if he were still performing. One school of thought states that he would have trouble hitting .250. And when doubters in the audience ask, "Why only .250?" the answer provided is, "Well, you've got to realize that he'd be almost a hundred years old."

MICKEY MANTLE:
Most Home Runs by a Switch-Hitter

Perhaps Mickey Mantle's father had a crystal ball. For Mutt Mantle, who died of Hodgkin's disease just about a year after his son reached the major leagues, ordered a baseball cap for the young Mantle when he was an infant and had Mickey dressed in a complete baseball uniform when he was just six years old.

A worker in the lead mines of Commerce, Oklahoma, Mutt Mantle raised Mickey to be a big league star and a switch-hitter. Mutt threw to his son right-handed so that Mickey would bat left-handed, and then Mutt had his own father throw left-handed so that young Mickey would bat right-handed. The youth balked at his father's switch-hitting demands, but Mutt persisted and told friends: "Mickey will be the best switch-hitter that ever lived if I have my way."

In 1951, in the last year Joe DiMaggio played as a New York Yankee, twenty-year-old Mickey Mantle began his major league career. He played on through pain and pressure through eighteen brilliant seasons. He was a blend of speed and power—he could reach first base batting left-handed in just 3.1 seconds or smash the ball into the distant reaches of ball parks for what writers referred to as "tape-measure shots." He did all of this despite operations twice on his right knee, which finally developed arthritis; a broken foot and several broken fingers; operations on his left knee; various thigh and groin tears; and a chronic case of osteomyelitis that he contracted when kicked in the leg during a high school football game.

Mantle smashed 536 regular-season home runs, more than any other switch-hitter in history, and eighteen more in World Series games, more than any other player in history.

The powerfully built slugger recorded fifty-four home runs in 1961, most for a switch-hitter in a season in history. The year before he had recorded forty homers. The two-season total of ninety-four gave him another line in the record books—most home runs for a switch-hitter in two consecutive seasons.

Other marks held by Mantle include: highest slugging average for one season by a switch-hitter (.705 in 1956); most home runs in one month by a switch-hitter (sixteen in May 1956); most home runs in a season on the road by a switch-hitter (thirty in 1961); most total bases by a switch-hitter in a season (376 in 1956); most walks in a season by a switch-hitter (146 in 1957); and most runs batted in in a season by a switch-hitter (130 in 1956).

There was always speculation about how much more Mantle might have accomplished had he played without all those injuries. There is really no need to speculate. He was great enough, and few would argue that he was not the best of all the talented switch-hitters that have performed through all the years in the national pastime.

Mantle, whom Enos Slaughter called "the greatest one-legged player I ever saw," was honored at Yankee Stadium on June 8, 1969, and told the crowd: "I've always wondered how a man who was dying could stand here and say he was the luckiest man in the world. Now I know how Lou Gehrig felt."

BABE RUTH:
Most Walks in a Career

The stereotyped image of Babe Ruth—feast or famine, home run or strikeout—is destroyed when one notes that at the top of the list of all-time walks is George Herman Ruth. The Yankee legend, a slugger but also a smart team player, walked 2,056 times in his career, or approximately once every four at bats.

Even with Gehrig behind him, rival pitchers worked around the Babe or simply put him on base rather than face his awesome bat. Eleven times Ruth led the American League in walks, an all-time record. In 1923, he was walked 170 times, another all-time record, and reached base that season 379 times, still another all-time record.

Together with Ted Williams, Ruth holds the record for leading the league in walks the most times consecutively (four). And no player in history ever compiled as many 100-plus seasons of bases on balls as Ruth did (thirteen). Mel Ott with ten seasons of 100 or more walks is the closest runner-up.

The only other player in history to walk more than

2,000 times in his career was Ted Williams (2,019). Mel Ott is the National League leader with 1,708. And Hank Aaron, the man who broke Ruth's career home run record, is in sixteenth place on the all-time list of bases on balls with 1,402.

JOE SEWELL:
The Toughest Strikeout

The Sewell brothers of Titus, Alabama, rank among the most famous of brother teams that have played major league baseball. Of the three, Joe, Luke and Tommy, it was Joe who had the best career.

Joe was a top infielder from 1920 to 1933 with the Cleveland Indians and New York Yankees. He recorded a lifetime average of .312—failing to bat over .300 only four times. In 1977, he was admitted to the Hall of Fame.

His greatest accomplishment was his ability to avoid being struck out. The little infielder came to bat 7,132 times during his fourteen-year career and was fanned just 114 times. He was, as they say, a true contact hitter.

Sewell went through the entire 1932 season collecting 503 at bats and no strikeouts. Three times in his career he struck out just once in a season. His worst strikeout year was 1924. He batted .324 and posted a career high in strikeouts—seventeen, a figure players like Dave Kingman are capable of exceeding in a week.

Just how good an eye Sewell possessed is revealed by his strikeouts-to-walks ratio: 114 career strikeouts as opposed to 844 lifetime walks. Sewell's career strikeout ratio is 62.6. He is the all-time leader in that category. Lloyd Waner, a pretty tough out, is in second place with 173 strikeouts in 7,772 at bats and a 44.9 ratio.

HANK AARON:
Batted into Most Double Plays

Perhaps it was because he played for so many years and logged so many at bats and came out swinging, but strangely Hank Aaron tops the list of players who excelled at hitting into double plays.

In 12,364 career at bats, the right-handed-hitting Aaron was victimized by 328 double plays. In effect, almost three of each ten at bats saw the home run king doubled up. Brooks Robinson is in second place on the all-time list with 297 double plays in 10,655 at bats. Among active players, three have a chance to break Aaron's record: Carl Yastrzemski, Rusty Staub and Tony Perez.

DAVE NICHOLSON:
The Easiest Strikeout

Dave Nicholson performed for parts of seven seasons during the 1960s. In 538 games totaling 1,419 at bats he struck out 573 times. No player in history (according to a statistical view) was an easier strikeout over a career. Nicholson fanned 40 percent of the time he came to the plate.

A six-foot-two, 215-pound free-swinger, the St. Louis–born Nicholson averaged more than a strikeout a game. His top negative year was 1963, when he was a member of the Chicago White Sox. Nicholson played in 126 games and led the league in strikeouts with 175. He batted .229 that season and recorded twenty-two home runs.

Even players such as Dave Kingman and Reggie Jackson (who in 1982 became the all-time strikeout leader) tarry far behind Nicholson's career strikeout ratio proficiency.

In 1979, Gorman Thomas fanned 175 times to tie Nicholson's single-season American League strikeout record. The all-time leader for strikeouts in a season was Bobby Bonds. He struck out 189 times as a member of the 1970 San Francisco Giants.

GEORGE WATKINS:
Highest Rookie Season Batting and Slugging Average

A member of the 1930 St. Louis Cardinals, George Watkins played in 119 games and recorded a .373 batting average and a .621 slugging mark. The left-handed hitter notched seventeen home runs and drove in eighty-seven runs. His batting and slugging averages rank as the highest ever achieved by a rookie in all the years baseball has been played.

Not exactly a flash in the pan, Watkins nevertheless was never again able to come close to his rookie form. In his third season he batted .312. He wound up with a seven-year career batting average of .288.

Jimmy Williams of the 1899 Pittsburgh team and Lloyd Waner of the 1927 Pittsburgh team (both with .355 averages) rank second in the list of highest batting averages compiled by a rookie.

Lowest Team Batting Average

Ineptitude at bat has characterized many teams in all the years that baseball has been played, but the club that walks away with top honors in this category is the Chicago White Sox squad of 1910. Its collective batting average was .2117—the lowest of any team in history.

Runner-up teams include: Brooklyn (1908), .2131; the 1968 Yankees, .2141; the 1963 Giants, .2188; the 1971 Expos, .2291; and the 1969 Padres, .2245.

The 1910 White Sox, however, were in a class by themselves as far as weak hitting was concerned. The team had the lowest slugging average in history (.2614), and the second fewest hits (1,061); only the 1908 Brooklyn team with 1,044 had less. With 1,310 total bases, 179 long hits and 116 doubles, the 1910 White Sox stand at the all-time top of the list of ineptitude.

Despite its lack of punch—its record of seven team home runs was the league's lowest—the White Sox managed to finish in sixth place, and one can only wonder what the team might have been able to accomplish if its hitting had measured up to its pitching.

The Chicago pitching staff yielded collectively just 2.01 runs per game to rank second in the league in that category. The twenty-three shutouts hurled by White Sox pitchers placed the staff in second place—one shutout behind league-leading Philadelphia. It was a staff anchored by Ed Walsh, a twenty-game loser with a league-leading 1.27 earned run average.

The Best Lineup: The 1927 New York Yankees

The 1927 New York Yankees played 154 games and won 110 of them, finishing nineteen games in front in the American League pennant race. They went on to wreck the Pittsburgh Pirates in four straight games in the World Series.

They were known as Murderers' Row, and they proved it day after day across the 1927 season. The Yankee lineup included Babe Ruth, who slammed sixty home runs in the regular season and two more in the World Series, as well as Most Valuable Player Lou Gehrig, who hit forty-seven home runs, drove in 175 runs, and notched 447 total bases. He finished second to Ruth with a .765 slugging percentage.

The Yankees also had Earl Combs, the league leader in hits, singles and triples, and Tony Lazzeri and Bob Meusel, both of whom finished among the league's top four base stealers, adding dash to the Bronx Bomber firepower. Five Yankee regulars batted .300 or better; four regulars drove in 100 or more runs. The team's slugging average was an astonishing .4890—highest of any club in history.

The lefty power duo of Ruth (who batted third) and Gehrig (who batted fourth) accounted for 107 home runs—

just sixty-nine less than the rest of the entire American League. Between them, they drove in a collective 399 runs.

Tony Lazzeri batted .309 and Bob Meusel batted .337. Their combined twenty-six home runs made them the best right-handed power pair in the American League. Third in total bases with 331, Earl Combs was the most effective lead-off man in the league. He was first among all American League players in hits (231), triples (twenty-three) and times at bat (648).

Shortstop Mark Koenig batted .285; third baseman Joe Dugan was a .269 batter, and catchers Pat Collins at .275 and Johnny Grabowski at .277 provided no relief for opposing pitchers.

A Yankee was the leader in each major offensive category except for stolen bases and doubles. The team batting average was .307, first among all clubs; the Yankees scored 975 runs to lead all American League teams, and slammed 158 home runs. The runnerup Philadelphia Athletics managed just fifty-six home runs as a team.

Perhaps the most underrated performer in the Yankee lineup was Bob Meusel. Dubbed Silent Bob because of his taciturn nature, he had one of the best throwing arms of all left fielders. He batted behind Ruth and Gehrig and still was able to drive in 103 runs. His .337 batting average was his best season mark.

Lazzeri's eighteen home runs placed him third in the league, behind his teammates Ruth and Gehrig, and the steady second baseman also batted .309 and managed to drive in 102 runs. One can only wonder how many more he would have had if he had not batted behind Ruth, Gehrig, and Meusel.

The offensive explosiveness of the 1927 Yankees was symbolized on different occasions by a three-triple day by Combs, a three-home-run day by Lazzeri, a three-home-run day by Gehrig, the first home run in history ever hit into the enlarged pavilion in right field at Comiskey Park (smashed by Gehrig), and the first home run to be hit out of the expanded Comiskey Park (smashed by Ruth). The awesome lineup pounded pitchers day after day, and it was not until a game in early September that it was finally shut out, 1–0, by Lefty Grove of Philadelphia.

The seventh-place St. Louis Browns lost twenty-one games in a row to the Yankees and avoided a season's sweep with a victory in the last game played between the two teams. The Browns won that game, 1–0.

The pulverizing power of the Yankee lineup enabled them to remain in first place each day of the 1927 season. The team had won twenty-three of thirty-three games played as May came to a close. A Fourth of July doubleheader romp over Washington saw the Yanks score thirty runs to the Senators' two. The pounding pushed the Bronx Bombers' lead to 11½ games. On September 13, the Yankees clinched the pennant.

It was a team that was called Window-Breakers and Murderers' Row. It was probably the most potent lineup ever sent to the plate.

TRIS SPEAKER:
Most Career Doubles

Hall of Fame Tris Speaker played in the majors for twenty-two seasons. Fifth on the all-time list in hits, seventh in triples, eighth in runs batted in, seventh in batting average, the graceful center fielder stands all alone as the player with the most doubles in the history of baseball— 793. Stan Musial with 725 and Ty Cobb with 724 are his closest competitors.

Speaker's nickname was the Gray Eagle. The title came as a result of the unique way in which he played his position in the field. He would play very shallow and race back to swoop down on fly balls hit over his head like some mighty eagle going after his prey.

However, it was as a two-base hit specialist that Speaker really excelled. Eight times the slash-hitting southpaw led the American League in doubles. In effect, of Speaker's 3,515 hits, 23 percent were doubles.

Other Speaker two-base hit records include a tie for the all-time lead for most seasons leading the league in doubles (eight) and the most seasons leading the league consecutively, (four). Five times Speaker had seasons of more than fifty doubles a year—he is the all-time leader in this category.

With all of his records for doubles, Speaker still had to take a back seat for the most doubles in one season to Earl Webb of the Boston Red Sox. Webb collected sixty-seven in 1931. Speaker's best mark was fifty-nine in 1923.

SAM CRAWFORD:
Most Career Triples

Sam Crawford recorded 312 triples in a nineteen-year playing career that began in 1899 with the Cincinnati Reds and concluded in 1917 with the Detroit Tigers. A left-handed-hitting outfielder, admitted to baseball's Hall of Fame in 1957, Crawford set records for most times leading the major leagues in triples (five) and most seasons leading the league in triples (six).

Dubbed Wahoo Sam (he grew up in Wahoo, Nebraska), Crawford played in the same outfield with Ty Cobb from 1905 to 1917. It was during those thirteen seasons that Crawford notched his personal high for triples in a year—twenty-six in 1914, tying him with Joe Jackson for second place behind Owen Wilson, the all-time leader who recorded thirty-six triples in 1912 as a member of the Pittsburgh Pirates.

Crawford also holds the record for the most seasons of twenty or more triples (five) and is tied for the most consecutive seasons leading the league in triples (three) with three other players.

The mark of 312 career triples is a mighty statistic; only Ty Cobb with 297 and Honus Wagner with 252 ever came close to it. None of today's major league performers are even in the top fifty as far as career triples are concerned.

Lowest Team Batting Average in One Season

The 1906 Chicago White Sox had a team batting average of .230. It was the most anemic mark of any baseball team that year, but the team's pitching more than made up for its lack of hitting. The White Sox staff recorded shutouts in thirty-two of the team's ninety-three victories. The Hitless Wonders won the American League pennant and faced the Chicago Cubs in the World Series. The Hitless Wonders continued their winning ways in the World Series by trimming their crosstown rivals in six games.

In 1910, the weak-hitting White Sox outdid themselves. They batted a puny .211—the lowest team batting average in a season in baseball history. They were not "wonders" that year as they finished in sixth place behind the Philadelphia Athletics. Chicago scored just 456 runs, managed just seven home runs as a team, and compiled a puny slugging average of .261. Its eight regulars had the following batting averages: 1B C. Gandil (.193); 2B R. Zeider (.217); SS L. Blackburne (.174); 3B B. Purtell (.234); RF S. Collins (.197); CF P. Meloan (.243); LF P. Dougherty (.248); and C F. Payne (.218).

Other teams who came close but never quite topped

the White Sox lack of batting punch include Brooklyn in 1908 (.213); the Yankees in 1968 (.214); the Giants in 1963 (.218); San Diego in 1969 (.224), and Milwaukee in 1971 (.229).

The 1910 White Sox set a few other records for futility at the plate: fewest long hits ever (179); fewest total bases (1,310), and fewest hits in a season in American League history (1,061). The 1908 Brooklyn team has the all-time record. They managed to get through their season on just 1,044 hits but batted two points higher as a team than the 1910 White Sox.

PHIL RIZZUTO:
Best Bunter

Born September 25,1918, in Brooklyn, New York, Phil Rizzuto was found wanting in a tryout by the Dodgers and wound up as a member of the New York Yankees. An acrobatic shortstop and a team sparkplug, the Scooter performed in pinstripes for thirteen seasons and earned a reputation as one of the most adept bat handlers of his time.

From 1949 to 1952, Rizzuto led the majors in sacrifice hits—and no player in history has ever equaled that feat of four campaigns of bunt magic, much less done it in four straight seasons.

No less a baseball authority than Ty Cobb called Rizzuto "one of the best bunters of all time." One of the most memorable moments of bunting for Rizzuto took place on September 17, 1951, in a game against Cleveland, with whom the Yankees were battling for first place. Rizzuto's suicide squeeze in the bottom of the ninth inning scored Joe DiMaggio and gave the Yanks a 2–1 triumph that enabled the Bronx Bombers to take possession of first place—a position they never relinquished for the rest of the season. Rizzuto bunted a high and inside pitch—one that few batters could have handled—and bunted it perfectly to bring in DiMag.

He batted a lifetime .273, but the average belies what Rizzuto's value to the Yankees was and what it would have been had he not been up so many times attempting to move along other runners by playing for the team and not for himself.

BILL BERGEN:
Lowest Career Batting Average

A major league catcher from 1901 to 1911, Bill Bergen has the lowest lifetime batting average of players with 2,500 or more at bats—a puny .170. The right-handed batter was a model of consistency. He batted .227 in his best hitting season and .122 in his worst year. Bergen was truly handicapped at the plate. He managed just two lifetime home runs, 516 hits, and a .201 slugging average in 3,028 at bats during his time with Cincinnati and Brooklyn.

TED WILLIAMS:
Most RBIs and Walks as a Rookie

There are all types of legends that have developed about the incredible eyesight possessed by Ted Williams. It was said that he could read the label on a spinning 78-rpm phonograph record. It was said that he was able to pick up ducks flying toward a blind long before the other hunters even realized they were there. It was said that when he was called out on strikes, movies would later show that he was correct in taking the pitch and that the umpires were wrong in their judgment.

Some of these legends may be true, but the indisputable fact is that Ted Williams was perhaps the greatest hitter that ever lived. In his rookie season of 1939 with the Red Sox, he revealed to all his potential as a hitter by doing something no rookie hitter before or since has ever accomplished: he drew 107 walks and drove in 145 runs. Both marks showed off his great batting eye and his ability to hit in the clutch.

"Hell," Williams recalled, "when I first came up I'd never even seen a big league game. I guess that insecurity was one of the reasons I was so brash. . . . But after I'd played in the American League one round, one series, against each team, I said—and you know I wasn't hitting that good, about .260—but I said, 'I don't see no blinding fastballs or exploding curves.' And I knew from that one round that I could hit in the big leagues. And from that July 4th on that season, I hit .380."

Williams batted .327 in his rookie season, and his 145 RBIs were first in the American League, his 107 walks placed him second. Through the years the only rookies who have come close to the records set by Williams are Jim Gilliam with 100 walks for the 1953 Brooklyn Dodgers and Wally Berger with 119 RBIs with the Boston National League team in 1930.

Joe DiMaggio rapping out another hit during his incredible fifty-six-game hitting streak in 1941. (Courtesy New York Yankees)

Don Larsen at Yankee Stadium on his way to a perfect game in the 1956 World Series. (Courtesy New York Yankees)

The final pitch being delivered by Don Larsen as he recorded a perfect game in the 1956 World Series. The young second baseman is Billy Martin. (Courtesy New York Yankees)

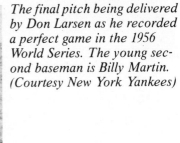

Jubilant battery mates: Yogi Berra and Don Larsen after the "perfect game." (Courtesy New York Yankees)

The Iron Horse, Lou Gehrig, in a moment of relaxation. (Courtesy New York Yankees)

Power personified: Babe Ruth in a follow-through after a mighty swing. (Courtesy New York Yankees)

Rickey Henderson, the greatest base stealer in the land, doing what he does best, running. (Courtesy Oakland Athletics)

Roger Maris taking it all in—the sixtieth home run that tied him for the all-time single-season record with Babe Ruth. (Courtesy New York Yankees)

Ty Cobb, the Georgia Peach, perhaps the greatest all-round baseball player that ever lived. (Courtesy Detroit Tigers)

The man who hit "the shot heard round the world," Bobby Thomson, one of the great favorites of New York Giant fans. (Author's Collection)

Hank Aaron watches No. 715 sail into history at Atlanta Stadium on April 8, 1974. (Courtesy Atlanta Braves)

Steve Carlton, the all-time left-handed strike-out pitcher and the only man to win four Cy Young Awards. (Courtesy Philadelphia Phillies)

Pete Rose, the man who proved that singles hitters can drive Cadillacs. Only Ty Cobb recorded more singles than Pete Rose, and "Charlie Hustle" is still playing. (Courtesy Philadelphia Phillies)

The awesome swing of Mickey Mantle, regarded as the most powerful switch-hitter that ever lived. (Courtesy New York Yankees)

Satchel Paige, the oldest pitcher ever to play in the majors, with Jackie Robinson, the man who broke baseball's color barrier.

*Three New York Yankees
who hold all-time rec-
ords: Phil Rizzuto, most
sacrifice hits in a season;
Joe DiMaggio, fifty-six-
game hitting streak;
Yogi Berra, scores of
World Series records and
catcher milestones.
(Courtesy American
League)*

*Reggie Jackson, a fine
player and also one who
has struck out more
times than any other
performer in history.
(Courtesy New York
Yankees)*

Ted Williams, the last player to bat .400 in a season, who in 1939 managed more RBIs and more walks as a rookie than any rookie before or since.

Lefty Grove, who led the American League nine times in winning percentage, more than any other pitcher in history.

Casey Stengel, who knew the glory of the New York Yankees and the agony of the New York Mets—one of the greatest managers of all time. (Courtesy American League)

PITCHING

Perfect games and no-hitters, hurlers who prided themselves on stamina and revved up relievers psyched to go all out for short distances, pitchers with overpowering "stuff" and those who pitched with their heads—all of this is the substance of the record achievements, streaks and feats of some of the greatest pitchers of all time. The following accomplishments are not described in detail but are worthy of special mention:

Most seasons leading the major leagues in games pitched:
    7—*Joseph J. McGinnity*, Brooklyn (NL) 1900; New York (NL) 1903–1907; Baltimore (AL) 1901

Most consecutive seasons leading the major leagues in games started: 6—*Robin Roberts*, Philadelphia (NL) 1950–1955

Most seasons leading major leagues in saves: 3—*Rollie Fingers*, San Diego (NL) 1977–1978; Milwaukee (AL) 1981; and most lifetime saves—301

Most seasons leading the league in saves: 4—*Bruce Sutter*, Chicago (NL) 1979–1980; St. Louis (NL) 1981–1982

Most seasons leading the major leagues in winning percentage: 5—*Lefty Grove*, Philadelphia (AL) 1929–31, 1933; Boston (AL) 1938

Most games won in a season: 60—*Charles "Horse" Radbourne*, Providence (NL) 1884

CARL HUBBELL:
Six Strikeouts in Two Innings in the 1934 All-Star Game; Most Consecutive Wins

---

A capacity crowd of 50,000 showed up at the Polo Grounds in New York City on July 10, 1934, to watch the second All-Star Game in baseball history. Many fans were jammed into the aisles, and almost 15,000 had been turned away when the gates to the park were locked fifteen minutes before game time. It was a crowd divided in allegiance. The American League team featured Babe Ruth and Lou Gehrig of the New York Yankees. The host National League team was managed by Bill Terry, who had led the 1933 New York Giants to the pennant. Terry, Mel Ott, Travis Jackson, and Carl Hubbell represented the Giants on the All-Star team.

King Carl, winner of a league-leading twenty-three games in 1933, started for the National League. Detroit's Charlie Gehringer led off with a clean single to center on Hubbell's first pitch. The speedy Gehringer wound up on second base when Wally Berger mishandled the ball. Heinie Manush drew a walk. With two on and no outs, all Hubbell had to look forward to was pitching to Babe Ruth, Lou Gehrig and Jimmy Foxx.

The crowd was screaming as Ruth strolled to the plate using his famous mincing steps. Catcher Gabby Hartnett called time. He jogged out to Hubbell on the mound. "Come on, Hub," said Hartnett, "don't mind about going to the corners, just throw that 'thing.' Hell, I can't hit it and they won't either."

The "thing" was a dancing screwball that broke away from right-handed hitters and baffled left-handed swingers. It was a pitch that had salvaged Hubbell's career, transforming him into one of the premier pitchers of his time.

Ruth took a pitch for a ball and then went down swinging at three straight screwballs. Lou Gehrig also took Hubbell's first pitch for a ball, and then went down swinging at three straight screwballs. The Yankee first baseman's strikeout swing was so violent that Hartnett was distracted and Gehringer and Manush were able to execute a double steal. Hubbell closed out the first inning's heroics by fanning Jimmy Foxx, who at least was able to foul-tip one of the three screwballs he missed.

In the second inning, Hubbell, a slim, sad-faced man

from Oklahoma, peered in against Al Simmons, who would hit .344 and strike out just fifty-eight times for the 1934 Chicago White Sox. Hubbell struck out Simmons with the screwball, and the crowd screamed for more. They got more. Hub fanned Joe Cronin for his fifth straight strikeout against five of the greatest batting stars in baseball.

Yankee catcher Bill Dickey snapped the southpaw's string with a single. But Hubbell fanned pitcher Lefty Gomez to cap his performance—six strikeouts in two innings. For years Gomez would brag about the honor of his "being in such distinguished hitting company" in the 1934 All-Star Game.

The American League went on to win the game, 9–7, but Hubbell's superb accomplishment that July day is what will be remembered. "We won," said American League All-Star manager Joe Cronin, "but Hubbell is unquestionably the greatest pitcher I have ever seen. He showed himself out there today. He had something no other pitcher has—a screwball, with which you just can't do a thing."

Reflecting today on his historic feat, Hubbell notes: "My career came hand in hand with the Depression. Ball players had to be dedicated. There were millions and millions of people out of work.... Those great hitters I struck out, and me just an old country boy, no one was more surprised than me."

Through the long Depression years, Hub was a constant in the shifting fortunes of the team that played out of the old Polo Grounds. His screwball thrown at different speeds blended with his dazzling change of pace. He could make the ball almost disappear. In his sixteen-year career with the Giants, Hubbell won 253 games and recorded a 2.97 earned run average. He was nicknamed the Meal Ticket because of his selfless devotion to his pitching craft and his team.

His twenty-four consecutive victories—a string that began with sixteen straight from July 17 to September 23, 1936, and continued with eight more wins through May 27, 1937—is a major league record. Only Johnny Allen (Cleveland, 1936–37) and Dave McNally (Baltimore, 1968–69) with seventeen consecutive wins ever came relatively close to the record achievement of the New York Giant immortal.

DON DRYSDALE:
Six Straight Shutouts and 58⅔ Consecutive Scoreless Innings

From May 14 to June 8, 1968, Don Drysdale of the Los Angeles Dodgers was about as perfect as any major league pitcher has ever been. The sidearming right-hander shut out the Cubs, 1–0, yielding but two hits, on May 14. Four days later he went the distance to trim Houston, 1–0, yielding five hits this time. On May 22, Drysdale hooked up in a classic pitching duel with St. Louis Cardinal Hall of Famer Bob Gibson. The Redbird ace yielded just three hits and Drysdale allowed five, but the Dodger right-hander was on the winning end of the 2–0 score.

On May 26, Drysdale again spun a shutout as he led his Dodgers to a 5–0 win over the Houston Astros. In that game played at the Astrodome, Drysdale was touched for six hits. On May 31, there was a 3–0, six-hit shutout of the Giants at Los Angeles authored by Drysdale. That game was played before more than 50,000 who jammed the aisles of Dodger Stadium cheering on the tall right-hander. The ninth inning of that game posed the most serious threat to the scoreless-innings-pitched string, which stood at forty-four.

Powerful Willie McCovey led off the Giant ninth with a walk. The Giant slugger had a lifetime batting average of .256 vs. Big Don. Nate Oliver came in as a pinch runner for McCovey. A single by Jim Ray Hart and a walk to Jim Marshall loaded the bases for the Giants with no one out.

There was almost total silence in Dodger Stadium, a stark counterpart to the numerous times in the game when the fans there had given Drysdale standing ovations. Now they sat, tense, concerned that the scoreless string would surely end.

Dick Dietz worked the count to two and two. Then an inside pitch clipped Dietz on the left arm and it seemed that a run had been forced in—and that the string was over.

However, umpire Harry Wendelstedt threw up his arms the instant Drysdale's pitch made contact with Dietz. The umpire ruled that Dietz had not made an effort to get away from the pitch and that the Giant batter had moved his arm in the path of the ball to make contact with it.

For more than five minutes the Giants protested the umpire's ruling amid catcalls and jeers from the stands.

"It was the best thing that could have happened," Drysdale later recalled. "It gave me a chance to catch my breath and collect myself."

When play was resumed, Dietz faced Drysdale with a 3–2 count. Dietz lifted a fly ball to shallow left field that was caught. The runners held. Drysdale then got Ty Cline on a grounder to Wes Parker, who threw home, forcing the runner at the plate. When Jack Hiatt popped up to Parker, it seemed all of Los Angeles exploded with joy. Fans jumped out onto the field at Dodger Stadium swarming all over Drysdale, pounding him on the back, screaming out congratulations.

In the safety of the dressing room, Drysdale was asked what he was thinking about when he went out to face the Giants in the ninth inning aiming to close out his fifth straight shutout. "I thought I wanted to get them out one, two, three. But instead I got them out with runners on bases one, two and three."

A Dodger publicist sent the ball that Jack Hiatt hit for the final out to the Hall of Fame with a note: "Don will be along in a few years." And Wes Parker revealed that he never even removed the ball from his glove after catching the inning-ending fly, nor did he touch it, but let Drysdale pick it out himself.

Even before he had started his record streak, Drysdale was outspoken in his comments about hitters in both the National and American Leagues. "They're stupid if they keep swinging for the fences," he snapped. "When they do that, they're helping me as well as the other pitchers. They're not just thinking right and I'm glad they're doing what they're doing. It's an accepted fact that good pitching will stop good hitting, and until the batters realize what they have to do to adjust, pitchers will dominate."

Having thrown down the gauntlet early in 1968, Drysdale then proceeded to back up his words with his powerful right arm.

His sixth straight record-breaking shutout was at the expense of the Pittsburgh Pirates on June 4. Drysdale shackled the Bucs on three hits as the Dodgers won, 5–0. His fifth straight shutout had tied the major league record set by G. Harris (Doc) White of the Chicago White Sox on September 12, 16, 19, 25, and 30 in 1904. Drysdale's sixth consecutive shutout set a new major league record and broke the National League mark of 46⅓ innings notched by Carl Hubbell of the New York Giants from July 13 to August 1, 1933.

"It's hard to believe I have six shutouts in a row," said Drysdale, who three times during the streak had survived bases-loaded ninth-inning crises. "Luck is a big factor in these things, and luck has been on my side."

It was much more than luck that enabled Drysdale to set the records he did. A durable and powerful student of pitching, the big Dodger ranks as one of the toughest of all competitors in the history of the game. Mixing a wicked curveball with a dancing fastball, when he was "on" hitters were just overmatched.

On June 8, Drysdale took the mound bidding to break the all-time major league record of fifty-six consecutive scoreless innings set by Walter Johnson of the Washington Senators, April 10 to May 14, 1913. Drysdale did not allow the Phillies a hit until he had assured himself that Johnson's record had been passed. That moment took place when Drysdale retired Roberto Pena on a ground ball to open the third inning.

In the fifth inning, the streak finally came to end as Drysdale allowed the first run to be scored off him in almost a month of frenzied competition. Singles by Tony Taylor and Clay Dalrymple put runners at the corners. Drysdale fanned Pena. Howie Bedell, whose total major league career stats consisted of three RBIs, managed one of them on June 8 against Don Drysdale. He lofted a pop fly to left field that enabled Taylor to come in with the first run scored against Drysdale in 58⅔ innings.

Ironically, 1968 was not really a banner year for Drysdale. He wound up with fourteen wins in twenty-six decisions, and the following season he logged a 5–4 record and retired from baseball. The streak, May 14 to June 8, 1968, was a time when all the magic was in his arm, the magic that enabled Big Don in his thirteen-year career to rack up more wins and more shutouts, strike out more hitters and pitch more innings than any other pitcher in Dodger history.

JOHNNY VANDER MEER:
Back-to-Back No-Hitters

"Records of all types are inevitably broken," says Johnny Vander Meer, now in his late sixties. "But what I did back in 1938 leaves me with the most joyous memories possible. It's a great feeling for an old man. I think that those two games will make people remember me for a long time."

On June 11, 1938, Vander Meer no-hitted the Boston Braves. And then on June 15, he no-hitted the Brooklyn Dodgers. No one has ever duplicated that incredible pitching performance—and every time a major league pitcher is able to toss a no-hitter, there is always that bit of anticipation prior to his next start. "Will Vander Meer's record be duplicated?" is always on the mind of those who follow baseball closely.

Born in Prospect Park, New Jersey, in 1914, Vander Meer joined the Cincinnati Reds in 1937. Vandy posted a 3–5 record in his rookie season and gave no real indication of the type of pitching he would engage in the next season.

On June 11, he spun his no-hitter against the Boston Bees, winning by a 3–0 score. Four nights later, he was tabbed to start against the Dodgers of Brooklyn in the first night game ever scheduled for the New York City metropolitan area. Only two pitchers to that point in time had ever recorded two no-hitters in a career. None had ever posted two no-hitters in a season. None had probably even contemplated back-to-back no-hitters.

More than 40,000 jammed into Ebbets Field to see the first night game, and Johnny Vander Meer in quest of his second straight no-hitter. Utilizing a 1–2–3–4 pitching rhythm that saw him cock his right leg in the air before he delivered the ball to the plate, Vander Meer powered a fastball that was alive and always moving in flight and a curveball that broke sharply.

Inning after inning, the Dodgers went down before

Vander Meer's moving ball. Not until the seventh inning did the Dodgers manage to get a runner as far as second base, but Vandy still had his no-hitter despite walking two batters in the seventh.

The fans of "Dem Bums" throughout the game cheered Vandy on, sensing that they were witnesses to baseball history. In the ninth inning, Buddy Hasset was retired on a ground ball. Then Vander Meer suddenly lost control of the situation. He issued his sixth, seventh and eighth walks of the game and loaded the bases. Cincinnati manager Bill McKechnie came out to talk to Vander Meer. "Take it easy, Johnny," he said. "But get the no-hitter."

Vander Meer worked carefully to Ernie Koy, who hit a ground ball to infielder Lou Riggs. The double-play possibility was there, but Riggs conservatively elected to go with the ball to the plate for the force-out. With two men out and the bases still loaded, Leo "Lippy" Durocher, a veteran of many wars, came to the plate. Only the Dodger player-manager stood between Vander Meer and the double no-hitter.

Durocher took a lunging swing and smashed the ball down the right field line—foul into the upper deck. Bedlam and tension intermingled at Ebbets Field as Vander Meer's left arm came around and delivered the pitch to Durocher, who swung and popped the ball up into short center field. Harry Craft clutched the ball. Vander Meer had made baseball history.

Fans leaped out onto the playing field, but Vander Meer's Cincinnati teammates formed a protective shield around the exhausted pitcher as he scurried into the relative calm of the dugout. Vander Meer's mother and father, who had come to see their son pitch with about

500 others from their hometown, were not as lucky. Swarms of well-wishers and autograph seekers milled about Vandy's parents, and it took about half an hour before they could be extricated from the mob of admirers.

The event remains in memory as the miracle of 1938—consecutive no-hitters by John Samuel Vander Meer, the man they called the Dutch Master. President Franklin D. Roosevelt sent congratulations, and newspapers and magazines featured every detail of the event for months. For Vander Meer, the double no-hitters were especially sweet coming against Boston and Brooklyn—teams he had tried out for and been rejected by.

In his double-no-hit season, Vander Meer won a total of fifteen games as against ten losses. His highest season victory total was seventeen in 1948, his next-to-last season. In 1941, 1942, and 1943, Vander Meer led the National League in strikeouts. He performed for thirteen big league seasons, winning 119 games and losing 121, and perhaps would be remembered as a southpaw pitcher who never totally fulfilled his promise if it had not been for the epic moments of June 11 and June 15, 1938—the double no-hitters.

TERRY FELTON:
Most Games Lost at Start of Career

"I keep throwing mistakes, and every time I throw one they hit it," said Terry Felton of the Minnesota Twins after gaining a place in the record books by losing his fourteenth straight major league game, more than any other pitcher at the start of a career. "I think I've got a snake around my neck, biting me every time I'm out there."

It was on August 11, 1982, that Felton suffered his fourteenth straight career loss, breaking the record of thirteen straight set in 1914 by Guy Morton of the Cleveland Indians. Morton's rookie-season record was 1-13.

"When I first heard about the record," said the right-handed Felton, "it was funny and I didn't really think I'd ever do it. I thought I'd get a win before I'd even get close to the record."

Felton's first career loss took place on April 18, 1980, when he lost 3-2 to the Seattle Mariners. On August 15, 1982, the twenty-four-year-old Felton was given a start against the Seattle team.

"I love to start," smiled Felton. "At least the game starts off tied." Through five innings, Felton had a no-hitter going and a 1-0 lead. In the sixth, Felton had lost his no-hitter, yielding two singles, but he was very much still in the game. With runners on first and second, third baseman Manny Castillo of Seattle smacked a ground ball back to Felton. It looked like a perfect double-play situation. Instead, as Felton recalls, "I messed up again."

Felton unleashed a wild throw over the head of Twins second baseman John Castino. In the confusion that ensued, one run scored and then another. Felton was taken out of the game trailing, 2-1. The Twins eventually lost by a score of 10-2. The loss was charged to Felton— his fifteenth straight major league career defeat.

Minnesota pitching coach Johnny Podres observed after the loss: "You get into streaks like his and you go out there on the mound and wait for things to happen to you. And they usually do."

"I try not to think of it," said Felton, "but somewhere in the back of my mind it's still going around. I could lose fifty in a row, and I'd still go out there thinking I can win the next game."

Manager Billy Gardner of the young and last-place Twins maintained he kept using Felton despite the losing streak because he had no one better. And Podres added: "Terry Felton has as good stuff as anybody in the major leagues. He's pitched in games and been outstanding. They couldn't touch him. But he's got to think low every time he throws a pitch. If we thought the next time he went out there he'd get another loss, we wouldn't bring him in."

Through his fifteenth straight career loss, Felton had made forty-six big league appearances. "Sometimes I just don't put the ball in the right place," said Felton. "Maybe I have to forget the rabbit foot and the garlic cloves and the horseshoes and just get meaner and meaner out there."

Felton concluded the 1982 season with an 0–13 record and a 4.99 ERA and looked ahead to 1983 and his first major league win.

WALTER JOHNSON:
Most Shutouts

A traveling salesman watched in awe as a big, right-handed pitcher struck out batter after batter on an Idaho sandlot. The salesman, a loyal fan of the Washington Senators, contacted manager Joe Cantillon and raved about the young phenom.

Cantillon dispatched his injured catcher, Cliff Blakenship. "Take along your bat, Cliff," said the Washington skipper. "And if you can get a loud foul off him, leave him where he is," joked Cantillon to his light-hitting catcher.

A few days later Cantillon received a telegram: "You can't hit what you can't see. I've signed him and he's on his way."

Walter Perry Johnson joined the Washington Senators in 1907 and remained with the team known as "first in war, first in peace, and last in the American League" until 1927. A nonsmoker and nondrinker, his strongest expression was: "Goodness gracious sakes alive." Batters had choicer words for the sidearming, whiplashing right-hander with the blinding speed.

Although Johnson holds the record for the most hit batsmen in history (206), he was too nice a man ever to dust a batter off on purpose. In that time before the use of batting helmets, Johnson always feared that with his velocity he might kill an opponent. Some players made a living out of this knowledge and dug in against him. "It was a disgrace the way I took advantage of him," said Ty Cobb, one of those who capitalized on Johnson's gentlemanliness. "Knowing he would not throw at me, I crowded the plate outrageously and hit the outside pitch more often than I was entitled to."

Johnson's record of 113 career shutouts—especially when considered in view of the overall ineptitude of his Senator teammates—is one of baseball's greatest records. The pitcher with the second-best career shutout record is Grover Cleveland Alexander (ninety). Johnson's shutout tally was considerably beefed up by the Philadelphia Athletics. The man they called the Big Train spun twenty-three career whitewashes of the A's—for more career shutouts by one pitcher against one team than any other hurler in history.

Once Johnson hurled a shutout on a Friday, another one on a Saturday, and another one on a Monday, three shutouts in four days. He probably would have had four shutouts in four days, but there was no game scheduled for the Sunday.

Twelve of Johnson's career shutouts were hurled in his high-water year of 1913, a season in which he posted a record of 36–7, a glittering 1.09 earned run average, and a record string of fifty-six straight scoreless innings—a mark later topped by Don Drysdale. So awesome was Johnson that Billy Evans, one of the umpires of that time, said: "Walter is the only pitcher who ever made me close my eyes."

Johnson's 3,508 lifetime strikeouts, 416 career victories (most in one league), and eight seasons of leading the league in strikeouts are a few more of the reasons why many consider him to be one of the greatest pitchers that ever lived.

Literally carrying the Washington team year after year, Johnson was selected fourteen times to pitch the Senator season opener. Seven times he pitched a shutout—another major league record. The Big Train was able to notch a one-hitter among the seven shutouts and hurl his Washington teammates to thirteen-inning and fifteen-inning 1–0 triumphs.

The magnitude of Walter Johnson's achievement is made clear when compared to that of some of the greatest pitchers in history:

Pitcher	*Career Shutouts*
Walter Johnson	113
Grover Cleveland Alexander	90
Cy Young	77
Eddie Plank	64
Warren Spahn	63

In the era of the relief pitcher, with fewer and fewer complete games being pitched, Johnson's total seems far out of reach today.

Some other stats achieved by Johnson include most 1–0 career wins (thirty-eight) and most 1–0 career losses (twenty-seven). The Big Train also has the most career shutout losses in history (sixty-five). In 1909, Johnson lost ten games by shutouts. It was a year in which Johnson notched thirteen wins as against twenty-five losses with a 2.21 earned run average for a Washington Senator team that won just forty-two games and lost 110 and finished in last place fifty-six games out of first. Perhaps it was that season's suffering that convinced Johnson of the need to toss shutouts.

HOYT WILHELM:
Most Appearances and Relief Wins

James Hoyt Wilhelm was born on July 26, 1923, in Huntersville, North Carolina. On July 21, 1972, five days before his forty-ninth birthday, his major league pitching career finally came to an end. The knuckleballing right-hander was one of the most unlikely candidates to inscribe his name in baseball lore as one who had pitched in more games than any other performer in history (1,070), and won more games in relief (143). And one can only speculate what he might have accomplished had he not come up to the majors at the advanced age of twenty-eight and twice had his right hand, his pitching hand, crippled.

"The credit for all my accomplishments," noted Wilhelm, "is the knuckleball. The thing with it was to throw it easy and not put a strain on your arm. You can stay in the major leagues a long time with the knuckleball. I proved that. . . . Just as long as you can do the job."

Wilhelm came up to the New York Giants in 1952 from Minneapolis. "Manager Leo Durocher had enough starting pitchers," recalled Wilhelm, "and asked if I wanted to work in relief. I told him that I would be glad to do anything to stay in the majors, and as things turned out that was the best thing that ever happened to me."

A six-foot 190-pounder, whose right hand had been injured during World War II in the Battle of the Bulge and was fated to be injured again later on in his career when hit by a ball thrown from an automatic pitching machine, Wilhelm seemed to thrive on adversity and tough pitching situations.

In his first major league at bat in 1952, he hit a home run, and he never hit another one in twenty-one years of big league play. However, it was his pitching that accounted for Wilhelm's longevity. In his rookie season of 1952, he saved fifteen games, posted a league-leading earned run average of 2.43, and recorded the league's best winning percentage, .883. Batters broke their backs attempting to make contact with his butterfly knuckler.

In 1958, Wilhelm wound up as a member of the Baltimore Orioles, and he credits something that happened there as another stroke of good fortune that extended his career. "Paul Richards of Baltimore," Wilhelm observed, "developed the oversize catcher's mitt. There were many catchers who had a lot of trouble holding on to my pitches. With them being equipped with that big glove they were able to hold on to what I threw, and that helped me a lot."

Alternating as a starter and reliever from 1959 to 1962 with the Orioles, Wilhelm won forty-two games and posted dramatically low earned run averages. In 1963, he became a member of the Chicago White Sox, where he remained until 1969. In three of those seasons in Chicago, Wilhelm averaged more than twenty saves a year. He closed out his career with the L.A. Dodgers in 1971–72, still tossing that hummingbird knuckler that he learned to throw those long years ago before several of the players on his final major league team were even born.

NOLAN RYAN:
Most No-Hitters, Most Walks, Most Strikeouts

The pride of the Houston Astros, Nolan Ryan broke Walter Johnson's career strikeout mark of 3,508 in 1983, but it will take some doing before another pitcher tops Ryan's record of five major league no-hitters.

Ryan's first no-hitter took place on May 15, 1973, as he pitched the California Angels to a 3–0 victory over the Kansas City Royals. Striking out a dozen batters, at least one in each inning, Ryan's no-hitter was threatened only in the eighth inning. Royals pinch hitter Gail Hopkins hit a looping liner to left field, but Angel shortstop Rudy Meoli made a spectacular over-the-shoulder catch of the ball with his back to the infield.

That first no-hitter occurred in Ryan's first season with the Angels. He had spent his first five years as a major leaguer as a member of the New York Mets. "I never honestly felt," said Ryan, "that I was the type of pitcher to throw a no-hitter."

On July 15, 1973, Ryan fanned seventeen Detroit Tigers and became just the fifth man in history to record two no-hitters in one season. Sixteen of Ryan's seventeen strikeouts came in the first seven innings, but his arm stiffened a bit in the top of the eighth as the Angels batted a round and scored five runs. "I honestly believe," Ryan said after the second no-hitter, "that it will be easier for me to strike out twenty than pitch another no-hitter."

In his final start of the 1974 season, Ryan hurled the third no-hitter of his career. The fireballing right-hander struck out the side in both the first and second innings and finished the game with fifteen strikeouts as batter after batter on the frustrated Minnesota Twins went back to the bench muttering about "Ryan's Express."

Ryan did some muttering, too, upset over his lack of control despite the fact that he pitched a no-hitter. The Texas-born athlete issued eight walks, seven of them in the first five innings. California's defense helped Ryan out as the Angels rolled to a 4–0 win.

On June 1, 1975, in his twelfth start of the season, Ryan moved into a tie with former Dodger great Sandy Koufax by recording the fourth no-hitter of his career. It was Ryan's fourth no-hitter in the space of just 109 starts. The victory was a 1–0, nine-strikeout performance against the Baltimore Orioles.

In 1980, the Houston Astros signed Ryan as a free agent and he returned to the National League, when he had begun his big league career in 1966. On September 26, 1981, Nolan Ryan pitched himself into the record books by becoming the only hurler in history to achieve five career no-hitters.

The fifth no-hitter was significant in many ways. It was Ryan's first National League no-hitter, and it was recorded against the Los Angeles Dodgers and helped keep the Astros in the running for the second half title in the Western Division.

Ryan wound up with eleven strikeouts (the 135th time in his career he had struck out ten or more in one game). He walked just three batters while throwing a total of 129 pitches (fifty-two balls, seventy-seven strikes). Retiring the final nineteen Dodgers, Ryan breezed to a 5–0 victory.

"The fact that the fifth no-hitter came in a pennant race, on national TV, and in front of my mom in the Astrodome," Ryan recalled, "makes it that much more significant. I've been there and lost too often to think about it before the seventh inning. But going into the eighth, I felt confident. I'm excited I was able to accomplish it, because it's the one thing I wanted to do since I got the fourth one."

No pitcher in history has a better strikeout-per-nine-innings-pitched ratio than Nolan Ryan. He owns the major league record with 145 games of ten or more strikeouts, plus the record for fifteen or more strikeouts in a game (twenty-one times), plus a couple dozen other pitching records. Seven times in his career he has pitched one-hitters. Yet, of all the accomplishments, the one with the most luster is the spot in the record book that says: "Most Career No-Hitters (5) Nolan Ryan."

On April 27, 1983, Ryan broke Walter Johnson's fifty-five-year-old career strikeout record of 3,508 to stand alone at the top of the list of all-time strikeouts.

Before the 1983 season began, Ryan was fourteen strikeouts away from the record. The Texas-born hurler managed a total of ten strikeouts in his first two starts. "It's been a buildup," he said. "I never realized fifteen strikeouts could be so hard to come by."

In the eighth inning of a game against Montreal, Ryan fanned Tim Blackwell on a 3−2 pitch to tie Johnson's record. It was his fourth strikeout of the game. Then he faced pinch hitter Brad Mills. With the count 1−2, Ryan served his ninety-eighth pitch of the game—a curveball. Mills went down looking and Ryan stood alone at the top of the list with 3,509 strikeouts.

"I don't get too excited about anything," said Ryan. "I was more relieved than anything else. Now I can sit back and relax and get more satisfaction out of it. It's been so long since Johnson pitched that I really know very little about him... only what I read in the newspapers."

It took the thirty-six-year-old Ryan sixteen full seasons and 3,357 innings to break the career strikeout mark of Walter Johnson that was set in twenty-one seasons and 5,923 innings. However, the fabled mark of 3,508 career strikeouts of Johnson and the new mark set by Ryan were fair game to be challenged in 1983. In third place on the all-time list of strikeouts at the time of Ryan's record-setting feat was Steve Carlton with 3,480, Gaylord Perry with 3,462 and Tom Seaver with 3,157. All of those pitchers were likely to add to their totals. Ryan acknowledged that he expected to be passed in career strikeouts by Steve Carlton who pitched every fourth day as opposed to every fifth day for the Houston power hurler.

With two pitchers past the 3,500 career strikeout barrier, it was clear that the 4,000 mark was clearly a record mark within reach.

BOBO NEWSOM:
Most Earned Runs in One Season

Bobo Newsom pitched in the major league for twenty seasons for almost as many teams. He began his see-saw career with the Brooklyn Dodgers in 1929 and was traded to the Cubs in 1932, to the St. Louis Browns in 1934, to the Washington Senators in 1935 and so on. When he finally called it a career in 1954, he was pitching for the Philadelphia Athletics for the third time in his well-traveled baseball life.

A broad-shouldered, good-natured right-hander, Newsom logged a 211–222 won-and-lost career record and a 3.98 earned run average. Only fifteen pitchers in history lost more games than he did, and only three walked more than Newsom, who gave bases on balls to 1,732 batters.

Three times Newsom led the American League in compiling the highest earned run average—he is tied with a few others as most proficient in this negative category. And there is one record that the itinerant pitcher has all to himself. In 1938, as a member of the St. Louis Browns, Newsom yielded 186 runs to the opposition, an all-time record. It was one of the most remarkably mediocre seasons any hurler ever had. Newsom won twenty games. He lost sixteen games. He started a league-leading forty games. He completed a league-leading thirty-one games and pitched in 330 innings while walking a league-leading average of a batter an inning. His earned run average was 5.06. The Browns finished in seventh place, forty-four games off the pace. They won just fifty-five games. One can only wonder where they would have been without Newsom's twenty wins (and sixteen losses).

DON LARSEN:
The Only World Series Perfect Game

On October 8, 1956, the New York Yankees opposed the Brooklyn Dodgers in the fifth game of the World Series. There were 64,619 in attendance. Today thousands more claim they were there. And those who actually attended and those who listened on the radio or watched on TV were witnesses to one of the peak moments in baseball history—the only perfect game ever pitched in the World Series.

Its author was Don Larsen, winner of seven of twelve games in 1953 with the St. Louis Browns, winner of three of twenty-four games with the 1954 Baltimore Orioles, the team the Browns were transformed into. Acquired by the New York Yankees in 1955, Larsen was transformed into a winner, victorious in nine of his eleven decisions. During the 1956 season, he won eleven games and lost just five.

When the Dodgers of Brooklyn faced Larsen in the fifth game of the Fall Classic, the knowledge they had racked the large right-hander for four runs in two innings in the second game stoked their confidence. But this was a different game, and a different Larsen. He walked no one. He struck out seven. He did not allow a run. He did not allow a hit. He was touched with perfection.

Like an old-time movie, the image of Don Larsen almost nonchalantly hurling the ball from a no-stretch windup to Yogi Berra remains in the mind's eye for many. The autumn shadows and haze at the stadium, the World Series buntings adorning the railings along the first and third base lines, the scoreboard and the zeroes for the Brooklyn Dodgers inning after inning... these images tarry, too.

The splendor of Larsen's accomplishment is enhanced when one considers the team he recorded his perfect game against. The losing team that went down inning after inning as Larsen just appeared to be having a game of catch with Berra was the Dodgers of Campanella, Reese, Hodges, Gilliam, Robinson, Snider, and Furillo. They dug in. They sliced at the ball. They shortened their swings. They attempted to wait Larsen out. Gil Hodges had recorded thirty-two home runs during the regular season. Duke Snider had led the National League in slugging percentage and in home runs and had wound up second in runs scored and total bases. Campanella and Furillo had collectively recorded forty-one home runs. Two of baseball's best contact hitters were Pee Wee Reese and Junior Gilliam. And Jackie Robinson, a symbol of determination and all-round talent, was still dangerous with a bat in his hand.

This assemblage threatened Larsen's perfection five times, but his invincibility on that October day remained.

Robinson smashed a screaming liner to third base in the second inning. The ball was knocked down by third baseman Andy Carey. Backing up the play, Gil McDougald was able to get the ball to first base just in time to nip the straining Robinson. In inning five, Gil Hodges slammed a Larsen pitch to deep left center field and was denied an extra base hit when Mantle caught up to the ball and backhanded it for the out. Sandy Amoros frightened Yankee fans in the fifth inning when he slashed a Larsen pitch into the seats—foul. In the seventh and eighth innings, Gilliam and Hodges returned to the Dodger bench muttering to themselves after being retired on nifty fielding plays by McDougald and Carey.

In his final three innings of pitching, Larsen seemed to grow stronger and stronger. The huge crowd at Yankee Stadium cheered each out. The ball park was like a huge radio speaker turned off as Larsen poised to pitch and turned on between each pitch and increasing in volume with each out.

The game moved to the bottom of the ninth inning. "The last three outs were the toughest," said Larsen. "I was so weak in the knees I thought I was going to faint. I was so nervous I almost fell down. My legs were rubbery. My fingers didn't feel like they belonged to me. I said to myself, 'Please help me out, somebody.'"

Furillo led off the ninth inning and flied out. Campanella bounced out. With two outs, Dale Mitchell, a lifetime .312 hitter, in his final major league at bat, came up as a pinch hitter.

Mitchell let Larsen's first pitch go by. It was outside—ball one. A slider evened the count. Larsen got the third pitch past the swinging Mitchell. The huge crowd was roaring. Yankee catcher Yogi Berra spit into his glove. Larsen prepared to deliver his fifth pitch to Mitchell. The ball came in and caught the outside corner of the plate. Mitchell hesitated—and was gone. It was a called strike three. Don Larsen had pitched the only perfect game in World Series history.

The six-foot-four, 215-pound right-hander, born on August 7, 1929, in Michigan City, Indiana, went on from that moment to complete a fourteen-year major league career. He won eighty-one career games and lost ninety-one and posted a 3.78 earned run average. But never again was Don Larsen able to reach the state of perfection he achieved on October 8, 1956.

JIM KAAT:
Most Years Pitching in Major Leagues

The Washington Senators are no more and 1959 was a long time ago, but like Old Man River, Jim Kaat of the St. Louis Cardinals just keeps rolling along. In 1982, the player they call Kitty Man completed his twenty-fourth season of major league pitching—an all-time record. Kaat previously shared the former record of twenty-three with Early Wynn.

A mild, gentle type, Kaat does not attach any special significance to his accomplishments. "As a baseball purist," he says, "you notice that baseball records are very deceiving. I stayed healthy through the years and was able to contribute to the clubs I played for."

One of a select few to play in four decades (the others include Willie McCovey, Mickey Vernon, Ted Williams, Early Wynn, and Tim McCarver), Kaat also sloughs off this accomplishment. "It's a trivia-type record.... If I had come up to the majors in 1960 instead of 1959, I wouldn't be one of those who played in four decades."

Nevertheless, the tall southpaw's accomplishments are indicative of his staying power and his overall ability through the years. Winner of sixteen consecutive Gold Gloves (1962–77), a three-time American League All-Star and three-time twenty-game winner, Kaat's pitching, fielding, and even hitting skills kept him around as an active player when other forty-three-year-olds talked about their memories.

As one of Kaat's former teammates said: "They don't keep you in the majors all those years because they like your looks. It's results that count, and Kaat has gotten results."

RUBE MARQUARD:
Most Consecutive Wins in One Season

In 1908, Rube Marquard was purchased from the minor league Indianapolis team by John McGraw of the New York Giants. The $11,000 paid for the tall southpaw was a record sum at that time. Marquard posted a record of nine wins and eighteen losses during his first three seasons with the Giants. McGraw's judgment was criticized, and Marquard was labeled the $11,000 Lemon.

But in 1912, Marquard accomplished a feat that no pitcher before or since had been able to surpass. In a string of pitching brilliance that lasted from April 11 to July 3, Marquard reeled off nineteen consecutive victories. He finished the season with a record of 26–11 and powered the New York Giants to the National League pennant. And all those who had called him the $11,000 Lemon now referred to Marquard as the $11,000 Wonder.

The closest runners-up to Marquard's nineteen-game winning streak of 1912 are Johnny Allen of Cleveland, who won fifteen straight in 1937, and Baltimore's Dave McNally, who recorded fifteen consecutive wins for the 1969 Orioles.

CY YOUNG:
Most Career Wins

His real name was Denton True Young, but everyone knew him as Cy, a name allegedly given to him one spring day when he tried out for the Canton, Ohio, baseball team. Young, frustrated with farming, was grudgingly allowed to pitch to the team's best hitter. Most of the Canton players laughed at the farm boy who wanted to be a baseball player. And the coach was so confident that his best hitter would smash each pitch that he didn't even use a catcher.

Young's first pitch was swung on and missed. The ball slammed into the fence behind home plate. Young's second pitch was swung on and missed. The ball banged a hole into the fence. Young's third pitch was swung on and missed and part of the fence fell down.

As the story goes, the Canton coach dubbed the farm boy Cyclone because of the devastation his pitching had done to the fence. And Cyclone became shortened to Cy.

There was nothing short about Cy Young's pitching accomplishments. A husky right-hander, Young began his major league career in 1890 and concluded it in 1911. And when he was done he had won more games than any other pitcher in history—511.

He posted twenty-seven wins for Cleveland in his first full season in 1891. The following year he won thirty-six games against just eleven losses for a league-leading .766 percentage and a 1.93 earned run average.

From 1891 to 1904, Young won at least twenty games a season—an all-time record of fourteen straight seasons of twenty or more wins. In his career, Young won twenty or more games a season sixteen times, another record.

The former Ohio farm boy recorded the first perfect game in the twentieth century in 1904 and had three career no-hitters. First in major league wins, Young is also first in complete games (753), innings pitched (7,356) and career losses (313).

In 1911, at the age of forty-five, he took the mound for the last time against a rookie pitcher named Grover Cleveland Alexander. He lost the game, 1–0.

Young was admitted to baseball's Hall of Fame in 1937. On November 4, 1955, he died, and the following year the award that bears his name was created. Each year the pitcher in the National and American Leagues who is judged to be superior to his peers is given the Cy Young Award—named for the man who was perhaps the most dominant pitcher in all the years that baseball has been played.

STEVE CARLTON:
Four Cy Young Awards

He's called Lefty by all those who respect the southpaw skills of a pitcher who looks like a sure Hall of Famer of the future. At the moment, Steve Carlton seems content to just keep on setting records and winning games for the Philadelphia Phillies.

In 1982, Carlton led the National League in strikeouts (286), shutouts (six) and complete games (nineteen) and paced the major leagues with wins (twenty-three). These stats enabled him to record his fourth Cy Young Award, an all-time record. Previously, Carlton had been tied with Jim Palmer, Sandy Koufax, and Tom Seaver, all with three Cy Young Awards.

Born on December 22, 1944, in Miami, Florida, the six-foot-five, 219-pound hurler was thirty-eight years old as the 1983 season began and a sure bet to battle

Nolan Ryan to become the all-time major league leader in strikeouts. He finished the 1982 season with 3,444, just seventy-four away from the magic mark set by Walter Johnson of 3,508.

Like the fine wine he collects, Carlton seems to get better as he ages. He is the all-time strikeout leader among left-handed pitchers and the National League record holder for the most one-hitters (six). Each game he pitches enables him to increase his records or move closer to another milestone.

HARVEY HADDIX:
The Perfect Game Lost

On May 26, 1959, southpaw Harvey Haddix faced the Braves in Milwaukee before 19,194 on a windy and raw night. Seven right-handed batters were in the Milwaukee batting order taking their cuts against the thirty-three-year-old veteran.

Inning after inning, Haddix was perfect against the slugging Braves, who had won back-to-back pennants. By the seventh inning, Haddix and Milwaukee's Lew Burdette were hooked up in a scoreless duel as rain fell lightly at County Stadium. It was a tense pitcher's duel, only Haddix was getting the best of it. At the end of nine innings, the score was still 0–0, and Milwaukee fans were rooting for the slim Pittsburgh left-hander. He had allowed no hits, no runs, no walks, nothing. He had pitched a nine-inning perfect game.

The contest moved to the tenth inning, the eleventh inning. The score was still 0–0. Haddix had done something no one before or since ever accomplished. He pitched a perfect game for eleven innings. In the twelfth inning, the standing ovations for Haddix became more frenzied. "I was out there," Haddix recalled, "just trying to win a game. The perfect game, the no-hitter, meant something, I realized it, but all I really wanted to do was win."

The Braves came to bat in the bottom of what would be the unlucky thirteenth inning. In the top of that inning, the Pirates racked Milwaukee pitcher Lew Burdette for their twelfth hit but could not score. Haddix, tired but still hurling with skill and determination, came out to pitch in the bottom of the thirteenth—to that point he had retired thirty-six batters in order.

Felix Mantilla reached first base on a throwing error by Pirate third baseman Don Hoak. The end of the perfect game shook Haddix, who still remembers the time with some bitterness. "It seemed to me that I had struck Mantilla out on the pitch before," notes Haddix, "but it was called a ball by the umpire and it gave Mantilla another chance. Hoak seemed to take all night with that throw—he seemed to be counting the seams on the ball—and then he threw it away."

Eddie Mathews sacrificed Mantilla to second base, and after Haddix got one ball on Hank Aaron, he was walked intentionally. Power-hitting Joe Adcock came to the plate. Haddix had struck out Adcock twice in the game and was bearing down hard attempting to notch another one. With a 1–0 count, "I tried to get a slider in on Adcock," recalls

Haddix, "down and away." The pitch was high. Adcock hammered it to right center field and the ball cleared the fence for a home run. The smash shattered the perfect game, the no-hitter, and placed Haddix in the record books with six other pitchers who recorded extra-inning no-hitters. Three of them won their games; the others, like Haddix, lost.

BOB FELLER:
Most Career One-Hitters

Hall of Famer Bob Feller pitched for the Cleveland Indians for eighteen seasons, winning 266 games—a dozen of them one-hitters, an all-time record. Only Charles Radbourne (with seven) and Steve Carlton (with six) ever came close to Feller's accomplishments—being one hit away from a no-hitter a dozen times.

In his major league debut, on August 23, 1936, the Van Meter, Iowa, farm boy, then seventeen years old, struck out the first eight men to face him and then seven more for a total of fifteen—one short of the major league record at the time. Feller's blazing speed and the power he was able to put on his fastball earned him the nickname Rapid Robert. In addition to the record twelve one-hitters, Feller also fashioned three no-hitters.

Most Games Lost

The pitchers who dot the roster of big losers range from a couple who were the greatest who ever lived to a mixed bag of not-quite-prime-time performers.

At the top of the list of big losers is Cy Young—the man who won more games than any other pitcher in history in his career also tops the list of all-time career losers. Young lost 313 games during his pitching lifetime. One of his closest competitors for the biggest career loser label is Hall of Famer Walter Johnson, defeated 279 times.

Perhaps the most lopsided loser was John R. Coleman, who lost forty-eight games for the 1883 National League Philadelphia team. Coleman managed to win only a dozen games that year. A workhorse pitcher, he completed fifty-nine games and logged an earned run average of 4.87. Coleman's negative stats are cushioned when one looks at the record and realizes that his Philadelphia team won only seventeen games and lost eighty-one, finishing in last place with a .173 percentage, forty-six games out of first.

This century's record for losses by a pitcher in one season is held by Vic Willis, a performer for Boston's National League entry in 1905. No stranger to a losing season, Willis had lost a league-leading twenty games in 1902 and bettered this record with twenty-five losses in 1904. In 1905, though, he was in bottom form. He appeared in forty-one games and lost twenty-nine against eleven wins. Actually, Willis was a much better pitcher than his record showed. The Boston club was plain miserable, finishing in seventh place almost 54½ games out. Traded to Pittsburgh the following season, Willis underwent one of the most remarkable reversals in baseball history. He won twenty-three games that year—the first of four straight twenty-win seasons for the powerful Pirates.

Other dubious-distinction-award pitchers include:

Russ Miller and Steve Gerkin both hurled for Philadelphia teams, and both lost twelve games in a season against no wins. Miller had his no-win season with the 1928 Phillies, and Gerkin set his record with the 1945 Athletics.

Right-hander Cliff Curtis pitched from 1909 to 1913 and along the way set the major league record for the most consecutive games lost, twenty-three. He accomplished this feat between June 13, 1910, and May 22, 1911, as a member of the Boston National League team. Curtis' 1910 record was 6–24, which placed him in fifth place among the all-time leaders in games lost during a single season.

John Nabors lost nineteen straight games for the Philadelphia Athletics from April 28 to September 28, 1916. He holds the record for the most games lost in a row in one season. He was 0–5 as a rookie in 1915, was 1–19 as a sophomore hurler, and appeared in just two games in his third and final major league season. His lifetime pitching record was one win and twenty-four defeats.

Even such stalwarts as Don Sutton can be included

among the ranks of losing pitchers. The Milwaukee right-hander holds the record for the most losses against one team in a season. Sutton achieved this mark while he pitched for the Los Angeles Dodgers. From April 23, 1966, to July 24, 1969, no matter what he tried, Sutton could not beat the Chicago Cubs, who defeated him thirteen straight times.

Statistics earned Hugh Noyes Mulcahy the nickname Losing Pitcher. His nine-year career won-lost mark was 45–89. One year he lost eighteen; one year he lost twenty. In 1949, he led the National League in losses with twenty-two.

JOE MCGINNITY:
The Iron Man

Joe McGinnity, who pitched in the major leagues from 1899 to 1908, was nicknamed Iron Man. The burly right-hander holds the records for pitching both games of a doubleheader lifetime (five) and most doubleheaders won in a season (three). McGinnity started 381 games and completed 351 of them. He had a career earned run average of 2.64. Admitted to baseball's Hall of Fame in 1946, McGinnity won 247 games in his career—an average of almost twenty-five a year.

In 1903, as a member of the New York Giants,

McGinnity won thirty-one games against twenty losses. He posted a 2.43 earned run average. He started forty-eight games and completed forty-four of them. It was in August of 1903 that McGinnity hurled three doubleheaders and won all six games. One of the games he helped win for himself by stealing home.

In his decade of major league pitching, McGinnity averaged 345 innings a season and a winning percentage of .630, one of the greatest pitching records of his time.

WHITEY FORD:
Best Career Winning Percentage Since 1900

Whitey Ford was raised in the Astoria section of Queens, New York, and was a sandlot star who just continued his development with the New York Yankees. And what development it was. A member of the Bronx Bombers from 1950 to 1967 (he was in the military service in 1951 and 1952), Ford was a study in steadiness and reliability.

He posted a 236–106 lifetime won-lost record, the best winning percentage (.690) for a pitcher appearing in 200 games since 1900. Ford's lifetime earned run average was 2.75. Three times he led the American League in wins and winning percentage; twice he led the league in games started, innings pitched, and earned run average. An intelligent southpaw, he changed speeds on his pitches and had fine control over a variety of pitches. "I think I could tell you just about every pitch I threw," notes Ford, "in the 3,170 innings I pitched. I was really into every game."

Dubbed Chairman of the Board because of his outgoing personality and classy manner, Ford was a businesslike type when he stood out there on the pitching mound. He had spurts of consistency that awed the opposition. There were back-to-back one-hitters in September of 1955; there was a streak of fourteen straight wins in 1961. There was a lifetime of pitching domination over Baltimore, a mark of 30–16 against the Orioles, best of any pitcher in base-ball history. His "feasting" on the Birds did much to fatten Ford's lifetime record won-lost percentage.

Just as his battery mate Yogi Berra holds so many World Series records for catchers, Ford tops the list in many categories for pitchers. He won more games (ten), pitched more games (twenty-two) and notched more strikeouts (ninety-four) than any other hurler in the history of the Fall Classic.

And although the Yankees through the years have had many great pitchers, it is Whitey Ford, the kid from Queens, who started and won more games, pitched more innings and compiled more strikeouts than any other pitcher in Yankee history.

FIELDING

The most amorphous of baseball records, fielding records are subject to many variables. Those who possess the best fielding percentages sometimes get there by "playing it safe," not going all out in their efforts to make plays in the field. Leaders in "most errors" categories often wind up there because they did overreach attempting to make plays that their peers would not even try for.

The whims and moods of official scorers, the kind of surface performed on (artificial or natural), the era a player performed in, the type of team he was a member of, the kinds of pitchers he fielded behind, the support he received from the other fielders on the team—all of these are intangibles in evaluating the greatest fielding records.

It is a category that has not been given all the credit it deserves by baseball people and fans. As St. Louis Cardinal manager Whitey Herzog said about his acrobatic shortstop Ozzie Smith: "He saves about a hundred runs a year and that ought to be as valuable as a guy who drives in a hundred runs a year."

On the pages that follow, a careful effort has been made to focus on the most relevant and representative of baseball's greatest fielding marks.

MANNY TRILLO:
Fielding Milestones

On Opening Day of the 1982 major league baseball season, Manny Trillo of the Philadelphia Phillies made an error on the first chance he had to handle the ball. Philadelphia pitcher Steve Carlton attempted to pick off Met baserunner George Foster on second base. Trillo's throw from second hit Foster in the back and he moved on to third base. Trillo was charged with an error.

From that moment on, Trillo played errorless ball at second base until his streak of perfection—eighty-nine full games and 479 chances accepted—ended on July 31 when he bobbled a seventh-inning ground ball hit by Billy Buckner of the Cubs at Veterans Stadium.

In the course of the streak, Trillo set the following fielding records:

July 17: Set a National League record for most consecutive chances attempted in one season and surpassed the mark established by Ken Hubbs of the Chicago Cubs in 1962.

July 18: Set a record for most consecutive chances accepted in a single season by breaking the mark of 425 established by Rich Dauer of the Baltimore Orioles in 1978.

July 25: Tied the mark for consecutive errorless games in one season, eighty-five, established by Ken Boswell of the New York Mets with 391 chances accepted in 1970.

July 27: Performed in his eighty-sixth straight game without an error and set a major league record for total chances without an error (459), breaking the mark set by Jerry Adair of the Baltimore Orioles in 1964–65.

July 28: Performed in his eighty-seventh game without an error to break the major league record for a season established by Rich Dauer in 1978.

"The ball wasn't that tough," said Trillo of the play that ended his streak at 479 chances and eighty-nine games. Trillo tried to execute a backhanded stop of the ground ball, but it bounced off his glove. He was able to pick up the ball, but bobbled it again and lost any chance of throwing out the slow-footed Buckner at first base.

"I think I should have handled that ball," said Trillo, not making excuses for himself. "It hit the heel of my glove, but in my mind it's an easy ground ball. And if I picked it up after missing it the first time, I'm going to still have an easy out."

The decision of the official scorer was slow in coming,

and the 50,203 at the Vet rose to give Trillo a standing ovation as he moved about in gloom around second base. Record setter Pete Rose said: "I knew what was going to happen. I said to Manny, 'Keep shaking your shoulders and tipping your hat and you're conceding that the streak's over.' I said, 'Quit it, quit tipping your hat.' I don't think Manny understood what I was trying to tell him, that the official scorer is sitting there and if he thinks everyone thinks the streak's over, he has no problem."

Official scorer Bob Kenney of the Camden *Courier-Post* first conferred with Jay Dunn of the *Trentonian* and then Larry Shenk, Phils publicist. "Emotionally, it was the toughest decision I've had to make in twelve years of scoring," said Kenney. "But I cannot score with my heart. I have to respect the National League caliber of player. I feel strongly it was an error."

The next batter was in the box before the scoreboard flashed "E-4." The huge crowd booed. Some of Trillo's Philadelphia teammates agreed with the crowd. "It's a bang-bang play," said Rose. "That's no error. That's a hit. I've seen a lot worse hits than that."

For Trillo, the end of the streak was in some ways a relief. "Breaking the record for straight errorless games in one season on July 28 seemed to be the most important at the time. After I got that I relaxed. Then I started to think about Joe Morgan's record—ninety-one games." Morgan's mark was set over two seasons in 410 chances from July 6, 1977, to April 22, 1978. "I thought," continued Trillo, "it would be nice to get it in one season since he did it in two."

Pete Rose, who played with Morgan at Cincinnati, said: "I don't compare guys, but Joe Morgan was and is the best offensive second baseman I've ever seen. Manny is the best defensive second baseman I have ever played with or against."

For Trillo, who set three National League fielding records and three major league fielding records, there was a whetting of the appetite to excel some more. "I'll just start again. It will be nice to break my own record now."

Unassisted Triple Plays

One of the rarest of all baseball records is the unassisted triple play. It has been performed only eight times in history.

The most recent triple play took place in Cleveland on July 30, 1968. Ron Hansen, a weak-hitting infielder who was playing out the string with the Washington Senators, was the unlikely hero.

A first-inning single by Cleveland's Dave Nelson and a walk by Russ Snyder put runners on first and second with no outs. Joe Azcue, swinging on a full count, lined a shot up the middle. Hansen gloved the ball, stepped on second, and tagged Snyder, who was scrambling to get back to first base. Hansen's heroics were "rewarded" three days later when he was traded to the Chicago White Sox. That 1968 season Hansen batted .185 in eighty-six games for the Washington Senators and .230 in forty games for the Chicago White Sox. However, it was the unsensational unassisted triple play that placed his name in the record books for all time.

The first unassisted triple play took place in the second inning in a game played at Fenway Park on July 19, 1909. Cleveland's Neal Ball, a slight shortstop who played in the majors for a total of seven seasons, was the star.

On October 6, 1923, in the fourth inning, Ernie Padgett, an infielder with the Boston Braves, made history as he executed an unassisted triple play in a game played in Philadelphia. It was less than a month after Boston Red Sox infielder George Burns performed the feat.

Pirate shortstop Glenn Wright, playing his second year in the majors, pulled off an unassisted triple play in a game against the Cardinals in St. Louis in the ninth inning on May 7, 1925. And Jimmy Cooney of the Chicago Cubs performed the rare fielding feat in the fourth inning in a game against the Pirates on May 30, 1927.

The one World Series unassisted triple play took place in 1920.

The fielder was Bill Wambsganns. In game five of the Fall Classic between the Brooklyn Dodgers and Cleveland Indians, Wamby made a leaping stab at a line drive in the fifth inning hit by Clarence Mitchell, stepped on second base for the second out and then tagged out baserunner Otto Miller, who had come down from first base and was standing next to Wamby in a dazed condition not realizing the game situation.

The seventh unassisted triple play in history was executed by Detroit's Johnny Neun, a day after Johnny Cooney's feat. The date was May 31, 1927, the first game of a doubleheader in Cleveland. It was the only time in history that a triple play ended a game.

No one has as yet managed to perform the ninth unassisted triple play in history, but if things go according to past form, the performer will be an infielder, and the three outs will be recorded swiftly.

WILLIE MAYS:
Best All-Round Defensive Outfielder

In 1951, Willie Mays joined the New York Giants. He was twenty years old. In a game played in Pittsburgh's old Forbes Field, Rocky Nelson blasted a drive 457 feet to dead center field. Galloping back, Mays realized as his feet hit the warning track that the ball was hooking to his right side. The ball was sinking and Mays could not reach across his body and glove the drive. Just as the ball got to his knee level, Willie stuck out his bare hand and caught it. Giant manager Leo Durocher told all the Giants to give the rookie the silent treatment when he returned to the dugout, but Pittsburgh general manager Branch Rickey sent Mays a note: "That was the finest catch I have ever seen . . . and the finest catch I ever hope to see."

Rickey was a fine judge of catches, but he didn't know what Willie Mays was capable of—and through his twenty-two-year playing career Mays made other catches like the one in Forbes Field and some that were even more incredible.

Only Ty Cobb played in more games than Mays and only Cobb, with twenty-four seasons as an outfielder, played more years than Mays. The lifetime leader in putouts by outfielders, Mays is second with the most chances accepted in the outfield, just thirty behind the leader, Tris Speaker. Four times Mays led the National League in double plays by an outfielder (1954–56, 1965)—another all-time fielding record.

Born Willie Howard Mays, May 6, 1931, in Westfield, Alabama, Mays was a natural. Five times he led the league in slugging percentage; four times he won the home run title; twice he was voted the Most Valuable Player. Winner of the Rookie of the Year award in 1951 and the batting title in 1954, the Hall of Famer was the darling of all Giant fans. New York Yankee zealots argued the case for Joe DiMaggio and Mickey Mantle; Brooklyn Dodgers rooters claimed that Duke Snider deserved more recognition. Willie Mays, though, running out from under his cap, streaking after a ball, firing a ball to the infield with force and accuracy, was the outfielder of outfielders. As fellow Hall of Famer Monte Irvin notes: "Having Willie Mays on your team playing center field gave us on the Giants tremendous confidence. We figured that if a ball stayed in the park, he'd catch it."

One of those catches that supports the claim that Willie Mays was the best all-round outfielder took place on September 29, 1954, in the first game of the World Series between the Giants and the Cleveland Indians. In the top of the eighth inning, Larry Doby walked and moved to second on an infield hit by Cleveland's Al Rosen. Powerful Vic Wertz came up. He had driven in the only Indian runs of the game to give them their 2–0 lead. He had singled in the fourth and sixth innings.

Playing percentages, Durocher replaced the starting pitcher, Sal Maglie, and brought in left-hander Don Liddle to pitch to the left-handed-hitting Wertz.

Liddle's first pitch was tagged to deep center field. Taking off the moment his instincts told him where the ball was headed, Mays raced back toward the bleacher wall. The ball was dropping in its flight, and Mays was running at full speed. Approaching the warning track, his number 24 lined up almost with home plate, Mays stretched out his arms as the ball went over his shoulder and made the catch. On the warning track, he whirled, twisted toward the plate, and fired the ball back to the infield. His cap fell off. He staggered to his knees from the maximum effort. The throw came in to Davey Williams at second base. The Indians did not score that inning. The throw and the catch would go down in baseball history as one spectacular moment. Its practical value was to ignite Giant momentum and enable the team to pull out a 5–2, tenth-inning victory and in the view of many change the whole direction of the 1954 World Series. The Giants went on to sweep all four games from a powerful Cleveland team.

The catch in the 1954 World Series, the rookie-season catch in Forbes Field—those were a couple of monumental moments in the fielding career of Willie Mays. However, the flash, the fire, the highly accurate arm, the homing-bird instinct for the ball, the speed to get to line drives in a hurry day in and day out—these were career trademarks of Willie Mays. Other outfielders came close to Willie's skill, but none had his combination of arm, glove, legs, instinct, desire and sense of timing. He was "the natural."

YOGI BERRA:
Best All-Round Catcher

When Yogi Berra first came up to the majors late in 1946, he was a catcher-outfielder. In 1947, he caught fifty-one games and was platooned in the outfield for twenty-four more. The following year he caught seventy-one games and performed in fifty others in the outfield. He didn't look like a Yankee, walk like a Yankee, or talk like a Yankee. "I want to thank all of you people," he said on Yogi Berra Night in 1947, "for making this night necessary." The comment was just one of the offbeat utterances that accentuated his off-balance image.

Bill Dickey, one of the standout defensive catchers in Yankee history, was retained as Berra's personal tutor. "Right now," Dickey observed, "Berra does about everything wrong. The main thing, though, is he has speed and agility behind the plate and a strong enough arm. I think he can make a pretty good catcher. Most of the others think he should play the outfield, but I'm convinced he can handle catching."

Oh, how he handled catching! An apt and willing pupil, Berra kept improving year after year. He became a top-flight catcher in all the categories that can be measured and a standout in the intangibles: leadership, handling the varied moods and different skills of Yankee pitchers, outsmarting hitters by either talking them into distraction or having his hurlers primed to capitalize on batting weaknesses. He played a portion of the 1949 season with a broken finger—and then later innovated the practice now followed by most catchers of keeping one finger outside the catcher's mitt.

Roy Campanella and Johnny Bench and Bill Dickey and others were superlative defensive catchers, but Lawrence Peter Berra did more of everything better for a longer period of time.

Inducted into the Baseball Hall of Fame in 1972, a three-time American League Most Valuable Player, Berra caught 1,696 games (seventh on the all-time list) in his nineteen-year career. One of four catchers ever to field 1.000 in a season (1958), Berra is in fifth place in career putouts (8,711) and chances accepted (9,619) for catchers. Tied with Gabby Hartnett for the most seasons leading the majors in double plays by catchers (six), Berra's 175 lifetime double plays rank him second on the all-time list.

One of his greatest fielding records is a string of 148 straight errorless games, a major league record. It lasted from July 28, 1957, to May 10, 1959. The streak of perfection saw Berra involved in 950 errorless chances—another all-time record.

Eight times he led the league in chances accepted, a major league record he shares with Ray Schalk. And just a few of the American League catcher records set by Berra include six times leading the league in double plays, eight times leading the league in games caught and chances accepted, and two times making unassisted double plays.

An excellent handler of pitchers (he caught Don Larsen's perfect game in the 1956 World Series and the two no-hitters hurled by Allie Reynolds in 1951), Berra bribed, badgered, bossed and got the best out of all the hurlers he caught.

Casey Stengel once noted: "I don't like them fellas who drive in two runs and let in three." He obviously was not talking about Yogi. For Berra did it with his glove and arm and bat. The vision of the squat, left-handed batter slugging one of his 358 career home runs or blasting one of his 1,430 lifetime RBIs is what made Yankee fans argue that Berra was the best.

His lifetime fielding average was .989. Bill Dickey those long years ago trained Berra in the intricacies of catching, and Yogi observed: "Bill Dickey is learning me all of his experience." Yogi learned it well.

Best Double-Play Combination

A pairing of second baseman and shortstop in temperament and ability has been the secret of defensive success for many major league teams. Their united skills and proficiency in executing double plays have snuffed out rallies and been billed as "the pitcher's best friend." Through the years all styles and types of double-play combos have attracted headlines, but from a purely statistical reference point, the best of all time was the 1966 Pittsburgh Pirate duo of Bill Mazeroski and Gene Alley, who combined for a record 289 double plays.

Alley was twenty-three years old in his third major league season. "Maz" was playing in his eleventh season and was but thirty years old. They plugged up the middle of the diamond, combining deft positioning with sure-handed fielding and accurate timing. Mazeroski's 161 double plays in the 162 games he played in that 1966 season are an all-time record. And Alley, who played in 143 games at shortstop, accounted for 128 double plays. The Alley-Maz combo erased the previous record for double plays held by Jerry Priddy and Johnny Lipon, who totaled 276 double plays for the 1950 Detroit Tigers.

Maz was no stranger to double plays. He combined with Dick Groat in 1962 for 264 and in 1961 for 261, placing his name in first, third and fifth place on the all-time list for double plays in a season.

Eight times Mazeroski led the majors in double plays, participating in 1,706 lifetime, both major league records. He was called Maz by impatient writers and official scorers. Mr. Double Play seems a more apt nickname.

First Baseman Fielding Feats

Perhaps of all the positions in baseball, first base has seen the widest range of fielding skills. Strong and durable

athletes like Lou Gehrig, slow-footed types like Ted Klu-
zewski and Johnny Mize, elegant and surehanded players
like Keith Hernandez, and fancy, stylized performers like
Ferris Fain have all held down the position through the
years.

There are various fielding records by first basemen that
underscore the different eras of baseball and the varied
kinds of performers at that position.

The best career fielding percentage for a first baseman
belongs to Wes Parker. A Los Angeles Dodger from 1964
to 1972, the switch-hitting Parker played in 1,288 games
and compiled a fielding percentage of .996. Steve Garvey,
Parker's successor, went on to set an all-time record of
his own. In 1976, Garvey played in 162 games and accepted 1,653 chances and committed just three errors—
the fewest errors in history in one season by a National
League first baseman.

The major league record for fewest errors in a season
by a first baseman belongs to Stuffy McInnins. A member
of the 1921 Boston Red Sox, the surehanded first baseman
played in 152 games that season, accepted 1,652 chances,
and committed just one error.

Jake Beckley holds the major league first base fielding
records for most games played, most putouts and most
chances accepted. And Mickey Vernon paces all players
with most career double plays for first basemen (2,044).

There are fourteen first basemen in the Hall of Fame.
The first three admitted were Cap Anson, Lou Gehrig
and George Sisler—and of the trio the former St. Louis
Browns immortal was the best fielder. The all-time leader
in assists for first basemen, Sisler was a dazzling blend
of agility, coordination and speed.

He is the all-time leader in assists (1,528). One of his most spectacular moments took place in a game against the New York Yankees. A ground ball was hit wide of first. Sisler scooped up the ball and tossed it underhanded to first base, thinking his pitcher would cover. When the pitcher remained stationary on the mound, Sisler charged after his own throw, caught it, stepped on first and retired the runner. It was reported there were those in attendance who thought Sisler should have been given an assist on the putout.

It's easy to start an argument over who was the best fielding first baseman, but for the vote for best all-round first sacker, Sisler deserves support. In 1922, he batted .420. In 1920, he batted .407 and also recorded 257 hits—more hits in one season than any other player in history. A lifetime .340 hitter, Sisler at bat or in the field was one of baseball's all-time best first basemen.

BROOKS ROBINSON:
Best Fielding Third Baseman

Graig Nettles is perhaps the flashiest and Billy Cox of the old Brooklyn Dodgers is definitely worth consideration, but a look at the record clearly shows that Brooks Robinson was the best fielding third baseman.

Born May 18, 1937, in Little Rock, Arkansas, Robinson joined the Baltimore Orioles in 1955 and was a fixture at third base for twenty-three seasons. Steady, cool, sure-handed and wide-ranging, Robinson recorded a .971 lifetime fielding average—the best of all the third basemen who have ever played in the major leagues.

He also dominates other fielding categories for third basemen, ranking first in lifetime putouts (2,697), first in games played (2,870), first in lifetime assists (6,205), first in lifetime chances (9,165), first in lifetime double plays (618).

A starter for twenty straight opening-day games with Baltimore, Robinson performed in more games with one club than any other player in American League history. In recognition of his special fielding skills, he was voted the Gold Glove award sixteen straight times.

LUIS APARICIO:
Baseball's Best Shortstop

Ozzie Smith, Marty Marion, Phil Rizzuto, Luke Appling, Larry Bowa, Dave Concepcion—the names of swift, steady, acrobatic shortstops come to mind quickly. However, a look at the record books reveals that of all of them—for longevity and accomplishment—Luis Aparacio deserves the vote as the best of all time.

He was called "Little Looie" and at five feet nine inches and 160 pounds, Aparicio was a small package of fielding fireworks. His career began in 1956 with the Chicago

White Sox and ended in 1973 with the Boston Red Sox. When he was through, he had played in more games (2,581) than any other shortstop in history.

The wide-ranging Aparicio ranks first in lifetime double plays (1,553) and first in assists (8,016). He is tied with Luke Appling for the most seasons leading the majors in assists (seven). No player in history accepted more chances at shortstop than did the Venezuelan-born infielder (12,564). Aparicio is the all-time American League shortstop leader in putouts with 4,548, just 591 away from Rabbit Maranville, the all-time leader, who played five more seasons.

Aparicio's fielding percentage lifetime was .972—good enough to place him eighth among the all-time leaders. Larry Bowa, Mark Belanger and Bucky Dent occupy the top spots in the all-time top fielding percentages for shortstops—and even in their prime they could not get near some of the balls that Aparicio was able to glove and turn into outs. From 1959 to 1962 as a member of the White Sox and from 1963 to 1966 when he was with Baltimore, Aparicio led the American League in fielding percentage—a total of eight straight years, a streak no other shortstop in history ever came close to.

Despite his fielding skills, his lifetime batting average of .262, and his ranking in ninth place among the all-time base stealers, Aparicio is not yet a member of baseball's Hall of Fame.

RUNNING

Rickey Henderson, Lou Brock, Maury Wills, Ty Cobb—
these are the names that are evoked when the subject of
great running ball players is brought up. Their records,
streaks, and feats are recounted on these pages. Others
deserving honorable mention include:

Max Carey: most seasons leading the league in stolen
  bases, 10 (Pittsburgh Pirates, 1913, 1915–1918, 1920,
  1922–1925); highest success ratio in a season, 51–53
  (Pittsburgh Pirates, 1922)

Davey Lopes: most consecutive stolen bases in a season, 38 (Los Angeles Dodgers, June 10–August 24, 1975)

Rod Carew and Pete Reiser: most times stolen home in a season, 7 (Minnesota Twins, 1969; Brooklyn Dodgers, 1946)

RICKEY HENDERSON:
Most Stolen Bases in One Season

Some baseball players have trophy cases that feature bats or balls or even gloves. Rickey Henderson has a shelf that showcases bases. Five bases occupy Henderson's trophy case. Two were inserted in 1980 when the fleet Oakland outfielder tied and then broke Ty Cobb's American League record of ninety-six stolen bases. Another base symbolizes Henderson's establishment of a new American League record in 1980. A fourth base represents Rickey's tying of Lou Brock's single-season stolen base mark of 118. And there's a fifth base for Henderson's shattering of the Cardinal Hall of Famer's record of bases stolen in a single season.

By the time Henderson is finished playing major league baseball, he'll probably need an entire room just for bases. "Nobody his age," notes Lou Brock, "has been good enough and developed the mental toughness and eliminated the word 'fear' like Rickey has. He has a baserunner's arrogance that is hard to get. And he has a burning desire for that moment when he is one step ahead of the tornado. He wants to become that tornado. He watches opponents' knees tremble and turn to jello. For a base stealer, that gives you strength."

Davey Lopes, a pretty fair base stealer in his time, offered this assessment of Henderson: "He's the most intimidating force on the base paths that I've ever seen. The difference between him and myself and Maury Wills and Lou Brock and any guy who steals a lot of bases is that he's much more aggressive and daring. That's the difference in Rickey Henderson. That's what separates him from the others."

Another thing that separates Henderson from the others is his age. The Oakland speedster was just twenty-three years old when he set the single-season stolen base record in 1982. Cobb was twenty-eight years old when he stole ninety-six bases in 1915. Maury Wills was twenty-nine in 1962 when he broke Cobb's single-season stolen base recording and stole 104. Lou Brock was a thirty-five-year-old in 1974 when he stole 118 and shattered Wills' record.

A turning point in the career of Rickey Henderson, whom Reggie Jackson calls "relentless in the pursuit of greatness," took place on August 2, 1982. Henderson stole his 100th base and became the first player in history to compile two 100-steal seasons. "I was pretty tight for that," said Henderson. "After the 100th, I figured they would start coming easy again."

On August 4, Henderson and his Oakland teammates faced the Seattle Mariners in a doubleheader at the Coliseum before a crowd of 19,526. Most of those in attendance cared little about the outcome of the games between the slumping A's and the listless M's. They had come to see Rickey run.

In the first inning of the first game, Henderson worked a walk off pitcher Jim Beattie. On the first pitch to Dwayne Murphy, Henderson took off for second base and went in with a head-first slide—his trademark. He had steal No. 101. The speedster attempted to remove the base, but had to receive assistance from a member of the grounds crew. Holding the base in the air, Henderson was all smiles as the crowd gave him a standing ovation.

In the second game of the doubleheader, Henderson beat out an infield single in the first inning and then took off on consecutive pitches by Rich Bordi, stealing Nos. 102 and 103.

"If there's a better base stealer, I haven't seen him," said Seattle catcher Rick Sweet, the man behind the plate when Henderson stole Nos. 100–104. "He put me in the record books."

Through the sultry days and nights of August 1982, Henderson moved relentlessly closer to Lou Brock's single-season mark of 118. "I used to be a crazy kind of kid," said Henderson, "and I guess this daredevil stuff is just a carryover. I'd climb up a tree and then fall out and then I'd try to climb the tree again. When I played ball as a kid in Oakland all I cared about was getting to the next base. I learned never to be afraid of being thrown out."

On August 26, in Milwaukee, with Lou Brock in attendance and hundreds of media personnel from all over the United States as interested onlookers, Rickey Henderson stole base No. 118 to tie Brock's major league record for most stolen bases in a season.

In the first inning of the game against the Brewers, Henderson opened the contest with a single up the middle. Mike Caldwell attempted to keep Henderson close to first base by lobbing a couple of soft tosses there. Rickey extended his lead—and Caldwell fired the ball to first attempting to pick Henderson off. Rickey took off for second base and slid head-first under the tag of shortstop Robin Yount, just beating the throw from Brewer first baseman Cecil Cooper.

"When I got caught off," said Henderson, "I said I'm going to second base no matter what. And I wound up just beating the throw." The 118th stolen base mark reached, Henderson leaped to his feet and raised his arms over his head. The crowd was cheering wildly. Henderson tipped his cap to the raving fans.

"I made a good move," said the southpaw Caldwell. "He was just too fast. When he was at second base, after all the noise the crowd was making died down I tried to get his attention. I winked to him."

After the game, Henderson looked wan and frustrated as he spoke to a crowd of reporters. Disappointed that he had not been able to tie and break Brock's record in the same game, Henderson said: "I think the mental aspect is the hardest in getting close to the record... and having to live with the pressure of getting the record for another night."

No. 119, the steal that broke Brock's record, came on August 27. With two outs in the third inning, Henderson walked on four pitches against Milwaukee starter Doc Medich. Four times Medich threw to first base attempting to pick off Henderson.

On the first pitch to Oakland third baseman Wayne

Gross, Brewer catcher Ted Simmons (who had been Lou Brock's teammate back in 1974) called for a pitchout. Simmons got rid of the ball quickly to shortstop Robin Yount, but the throw came in a bit to the right of second base. A head-first slide brought Henderson in under the tag.

The game was delayed for a few minutes as Henderson jubilantly pulled second base from its moorings and held it aloft for all to see. Photographers milled about taking photographs of Henderson and Brock, who formally presented the base to the new single-season stolen base champion in a ceremony at home plate. Simmons, Medich, and other Brewers joined with Henderson's Oakland teammates in congratulating him on his record-setting 119th theft.

Henderson set the record in 127 games, twenty-six less than Brock required when he stole 118 in 1974 with the St. Louis Cardinals. The 119th steal came on Henderson's 158th attempt, making the thirty-nine times he was thrown out another major league record. It erased the old mark of thirty-eight times caught stealing held by Ty Cobb when he stole ninety-six bases in 1915.

When he stole No. 119, Henderson's night's work was just beginning. He went on to steal second base in the sixth inning, and in the eighth inning he stole second and then third.

Medich, who walked Henderson three times and whose slow and deliberate motion seemingly was made for swift base stealers, had no regrets. "I'm happy," said a smiling Medich, "that Rickey got the record—he deserves it."

With the record in the books, Henderson admitted after the game that he was relieved that the media circus that had followed him about throughout much of the 1982 season was all but set to fold its tents. "To me," Henderson said, "it has been a lot of hard work, a lot of trouble on my mind, a lot of weariness. Now I can go out there and relax a little more."

Henderson finished the 1982 season with 130 stolen bases after breaking the single-season record for the third time in twenty years. In 1962, Maury Wills of the Los Angeles Dodgers stole 104 to break the record of ninety-six set by Ty Cobb in 1915, and in 1974 Lou Brock's 118 steals broke the record set by Wills.

For Rickey Henderson, as for Cobb and Wills and Brock, the single-season stolen base record may be a temporary thing. More and more speedy runners with daring styles seem to be entering the major leagues. Perhaps it was an awareness of this that prompted Henderson to remark:

"Every year I want to be a little better than I was the year before so that I can be the great player people are talking about every year. Right now, people always ask me about me doing what I'm doing at such a young age . . . but the main thing is that I got many more years to go and this is not the only thing I'm gonna do in baseball."

LOU BROCK:
Most Career Stolen Bases

In 1982, Rickey Henderson shattered Lou Brock's mark of 118 stolen bases in a single season, but the former St. Louis star still has a couple of incredible records in the books that will take some doing for Henderson and others to break.

Brock stands alone as the only player to lead the majors six times in stolen bases and the only player to record twelve seasons of fifty or more stolen bases. And the glittering jewel of all his baserunning accomplishments is his record 938 career stolen bases.

Born June 18, 1939, in El Dorado, Arkansas, Brock was three years old when Ty Cobb was elected to the Baseball Hall of Fame. In 1964, Brock was traded by the Chicago Cubs to the St. Louis Cardinals and encouraged to steal bases. He stole sixty-three in 1965 for a career total of 146 to that point. In 1966, he stole a league-leading seventy-four bases and in his own words "was off and running to learn all I could to steal even more."

A sensitive and intelligent student of the game, Brock explained that he learned daily through trial and error that "all you needed to know about pitchers was how to read them. Did they have the two-motion pickoff move to first base or the three-motion throw? What were their idiosyncrasies? As soon as you could read the pitcher well enough," continued Brock, "you could eliminate the catcher—he wouldn't have a chance of nailing you."

From 1966 to 1969, Brock led the National League in stolen bases. "The spotlight, the visibility factor," he explained, kept him going.

"I learned," said Brock, "that you could have no fear of failure if you were fated to steal a lot of bases. You had to have a certain arrogance. You're always on the verge of disaster as a base stealer. If you're thrown out you could be wiping out a big rally.

"Despite these thoughts," continued Brock, "you've got to have utter confidence in what you're doing and realize that it helps your team win games. You'll steal a base four of five times if you're good enough...and if they catch you, well, they owe you four."

In 1971, Brock became the first player in history to steal fifty or more bases in seven consecutive seasons. His career stolen base total stood at 501.

And he kept working at his craft. He figured to the tenth of a second the throws and movements of pitchers and catchers, the positioning of infielders, the habits of first basemen. Brock calculated just how much of a lead he would be able to take. He used a stopwatch to clock pitchers' movements. He even filmed pitchers in action. There was one time when there were many who thought the speedy Cardinal went too far.

During spring training one year he filmed pitchers from the relative safety of the St. Louis dugout, but he became so involved in his quest that one fair day he positioned a camera along the foul line to check out Don Drysdale of the Los Angeles Dodgers.

"What do you think you're doing, Lou?" shouted Drysdale.

"Oh, just taking some home movies," was the response.

"Get the heck out of there!"

Brock packed up his equipment and left, a smile on his face. "I could spend every night now with Drysdale," said Brock. "I had him and his motion stuck on a frame so I could study it—and there was not a thing he was able to do about it."

In 1972, Brock extended his record for most consecutive seasons of fifty or more stolen bases to eight. The following year he stole his 600th base and moved into ninth place on the all-time list.

Maury Wills' one-season stolen base mark was shattered as Brock stole 118 bases in 1974 and made a giant leap from ninth place on the all-time stolen bases career list to second place. "The ability to endure pain," Brock recalled, "was a big part of my getting those 118 stolen bases and a major part of the career record." There were times when Brock, who slid feet first and braced his slide with his hand, felt real pain. "The pain," he winced, "was so bad sometimes in 1974 that I could barely hold a glass of water in my banged-up hand."

On August 29, 1977, thirty-eight-year-old Lou Brock did some knee bends and walked out onto the field at San Diego Stadium. He needed one stolen base to tie and another one to break Ty Cobb's legendary mark of 892. Leading off the game for the Cardinals, Brock was walked by Padre pitcher Dave Friesleben. On the next pitch Brock took off for second base. The throw by catcher Dave Roberts went into center field. Brock raced around to third base, where he was mobbed by his teammates. He had tied Ty Cobb. The game was halted and second base was taken up and presented to Brock during a brief ceremony. In the seventh inning, Brock bounced into a fielder's choice. On the next pitch, the affable Cardinal took off for second. The throw by Roberts was wide, and Brock slid in under the tag of Bill Almon, who dropped the ball. Brock's twenty-eighth steal of the year put him one up on Cobb, who needed 3,033 games to steal 892 bases. Brock needed just 2,376 games to steal 893.

Ty Cobb's career stolen base record was regarded as the modern and official record, but "Sliding Billy" Hamilton, who performed around the turn of the century, was in the books with 937 steals. Critics pointed out that Hamilton performed in an era when scoring rules were a bit odd. For example, runners who went from first to third base on a single were credited with a stolen base. However, Brock acknowledged that if Hamilton had the record, he had earned it. "I'll do my best, however," smiled Brock, "to break it."

On September 23, 1979, in his nineteenth major league season, at the age of forty, Lou Brock stole No. 938 to pass Sliding Billy and all other base stealers who had ever played the game. Just a month before, he had collected his 3,000th career hit.

"The records," Brock mused, "made for immortality, and that was a part of my going for them the way I did." If, as the cliché goes, all records are made to be broken (and a couple set by Brock already have), he did in his time throw down the gauntlet. And those who seek to erase him from the books will need his drive, his talent, his staying power, and his pride.

TY COBB:
Thirty-five Steals of Home

Ty Cobb joined the Detroit Tigers in 1905 and batted .240. And then for the next twenty-two years he never batted below .300. With a bat in his hand, held in one of baseball's most unorthodox grips, Cobb was a threat to dump a bunt or slash a drive up the alley. Yet, it was his mercurial feet and sharpened spikes that made Casey Stengel remark: "Ty Cobb rules the field by awe."

Of all the records held by the man they called the Georgia Tornado, the one that most personifies his verve and competitive spirit is thirty-five steals of home. Eight of those steals enabled the run Cobb scored to be the margin of victory for the Tigers.

Not the fastest of runners, but surely one of the smartest and most daring, Cobb sought every edge he could find. He studied the movements of pitchers, infielders, catchers. He mastered a fall-away slide, making himself an elusive target for a tag. He had about a half-dozen different types of slides for all kinds of situations. He feigned injuries, changed his running pace, varied his leads and always came at those who would tag him out with razor-sharp spikes.

On July 12, 1911, against the Philadelphia A's, Cobb stole second, third and home on three consecutive pitches.

That was one of the three times he stole all three bases in the same inning.

Three times in his career he stole home as the point man in a triple steal. In 1915, he teamed up with Veach and Crawford; in 1919 he was part of a triple steal with Heilmann and Shorten; in 1927 he stole home as part of a triple steal with Simmons and Branom.

In 1915, Cobb stole ninety-six bases, six of them steals of home. On June 18, he stole home twice in one game against Washington. Cobb's first steal in the first inning resulted in catcher Dutch Henry's being forced out of the game with a Georgia Peach spike wound. In the fifth inning, Cobb once again stole home off pitcher Joe Boehling. The Tigers won the game 5–3, and the margin of victory was the two steals of home by Cobb.

"I was their enemy," Cobb said of rival players. "If any one of them learned I could be scared, I would have lasted two years in the major leagues, not twenty-four."

The worst thing an opponent could do was to call the fiery outfielder "lucky." The word sent Cobb into a rage. "I make my own luck," he would scream. He wore extra-heavy shoes during spring training to condition his legs for the runs and the slides. Once a season got underway, he would not attend to the scrapes and sores and bruises he picked up sliding ferociously into bases. "The skin toughens itself," he would snarl.

Cobb's steals of home symbolize his attitude toward the game. On June 23, 1915, Cobb was the runner at second base. Crawford was the hitter and tapped the ball back to the St. Louis Brown pitcher Grover Lowdermilk. An ungainly type, Lowdermilk had some trouble picking up the ball, and Cobb advanced to third. Then Cobb broke for home while the Brown hurler still held the ball in his hand. The Georgia Peach crossed the plate sneering at Lowdermilk, who was beside himself with anger and confusion.

Cobb's one World Series steal of home was against Pittsburgh in 1909. The runner on third base, Cobb watched as Victor Willis came in to relieve. He noticed the veteran pitcher concentrating on the batter and not on him, so Cobb broke for home. It was a clean steal executed before Willis even had the presence of mind to toss the ball to catcher George Gibson.

Cobb holds many records, but his thirty-five steals of home is one that probably never will be broken. The only one who came close was George Burns. A National League outfielder from 1911 to 1925, Burns stole home twenty-seven times.

DON BUFORD:
Most Difficult Player to Double Up

Don Buford performed for a decade in the major leagues, playing half those years for the Chicago White Sox and the other half for the Baltimore Orioles. At five feet seven and 160 pounds, he was a contact-type switch-hitter. Buford never managed to bat .300 in his ten seasons, but he was a handy player to have around.

His lifetime batting average was .264 and he averaged twenty steals a season, but it was in the area of not getting doubled up, not killing rallies, that he excelled.

Buford logged 4,553 career at bats and rapped into double plays but thirty-three times. These stats translate into the fact that Buford was doubled up less than 1 percent of the times he came to bat. It was his speed coupled with baseball instincts that made him the "tough" runner that he was.

FRED MERKLE:
The Bonehead Play

The phrase "pulling a bonehead play" or "pulling a boner" is part of the language not only of baseball, but of all sports, and in fact, of the language in general. Its most dramatic derivation goes back to September 9, 1908.

Frederick Charles Merkle, a.k.a. George Merkle, was playing his first full game at first base for the New York Giants. It was his second season in the majors, but the year before he had appeared in only fifteen games. The Giants were in first place and the Cubs were challenging them. The two teams were tied, 1–1, in the bottom of the ninth inning. With two outs, the Giants' Moose McCormick was on third base and Merkle was on first. Al Bridwell slashed a single to center field, and McCormick crossed the plate with what was apparently the winning run. Merkle, eager to avoid the Polo Grounds crowd that surged onto the playing field, raced directly to the clubhouse in deep center field instead of following through on the play and touching second base. Amid the pandemonium, Johnny Evers of the Cubs screamed for the baseball, obtained it somehow, and stepped on second base, and claimed a force-out on Merkle. When things subsided, umpire Hank O'Day agreed with Evers.

The National League upheld O'Day, Evers, and the Cubs, so the run was nullified and the game not counted. Both teams played out their schedules and completed the season tied for first place with ninety-eight wins and fifty-five losses.

A replay of the game was scheduled on September 23, and Christy Mathewson, seeking his thirty-eighth victory of the season, lost, 4–2, to Three-Finger Brown. The Cubs won the pennant.

Although Merkle played sixteen years in the majors and had a lifetime batting average of .273, he will forever be down in sports history as the man who made the bonehead play that lost the 1908 pennant for the Giants, for had he touched second base there would have been no replayed game and the Giants would have won the pennant by one game.

A sad postscript to the entire episode exists. The tumult brought on by the original game between the Giants and Cubs had emotionally affected National League President Harry Pulliam. He took a leave of absence from his position after the game. He allegedly went into a state of depression. On July 19, 1909, Pulliam committed suicide.

MANAGING

Perhaps the truest cliché in all of baseball is that "every manager is hired to be fired." Through the years there have been all types of managers: tyrants, schemers, cheerleaders, player-managers, those selected because of their popularity with fans and others put into positions of power because of their political connections. The Chicago Cubs once had a panel of managers. Alphabetically, major league pilots range from Bill Adair who managed the Chicago White Sox in 1970 for ten games to Don Zimmer who began his piloting career in 1972 with the San Diego Padres and is now a Yankee coach. Some of the personalities who have managed major league teams include: Ty Cobb, Lary Doby (Chicago White Sox in 1978); Cookie Lavagetto (1957–1960 Washington Senators, 1961 Minnesota); George Sisler and his son Dick Sisler; Honus Wagner, Ted Williams and Maury Wills.

Honorable mention for managing records should be given to:

Frank Bancroft: most clubs managed lifetime, 7

Danny Murtagh: most times managing the same team, 4 (Pittsburgh Pirates)

BILLY MARTIN:
Most Flamboyant Manager

As the 1983 baseball season got underway, the New York Yankees monopolized the Big Apple's media spotlight with an advertising campaign that raised the consciousness of fans of the national pastime. It was symbolized by the slogan "Billy's Back." For the third time Billy Martin became the manager of the New York Yankees.

"A sailing ship with no wind goes nowhere," said principal Yankee owner George Steinbrenner. "Sometimes you have to have a little turmoil," he continued, acknowledging both the talent and the tempestuousness of Billy Martin.

In 1969, in his rookie season as a manager, Martin led the Minnesota Twins to a division championship. With an aging Detroit club in 1972, he steered the Tigers to a division title. With an inexperienced and relatively talentless Texas team in 1974, he managed the club to a second place finish. He won the pennant with the Yankees in 1976 and 1977, and brought a young Oakland team to a divisional title in 1981.

As George Steinbrenner said after hiring Billy Martin for the third time: "You've got to go with a winner to have a winner. There are only two or three managers active in baseball who have winning records since they started and Alfred Martin is one of them. He has taken teams who had no right to be winners and won with them."

Martin's detractors feel that he showboats, that he loses faith and interest in players and teams, that he has sometimes been guilty of overreacting and too quick a temper. All these things considered—Martin is in the tradition of Leo Durocher and John McGraw—a bright, driven-to-win individual who today is baseball's most flamboyant manager.

CONNIE MACK:
Most Seasons as a Manager

Cornelius Alexander McGillicuddy, better known as Connie Mack, was a major league baseball manager for fifty-three years. He managed Pittsburgh in the National League from 1894 to 1896 and the American League Philadelphia Athletics from 1901 to 1950.

Mack holds the record for managing the most years in the majors (fifty-three), and most years managing one club in one league (fifty). He ranks first on the all-time list in games managed (7,878), games won (3,776) and games lost (4,025). Eight times in his fifty-three years of managing, his teams were able to make it to the World Series. Mack managed an overall Series record of twenty-four wins against nineteen defeats, placing him fourth in wins and fourth in losses on the all-time list of World Series managers.

Admitted to the Baseball Hall of Fame in 1937, Mack may not have been the best manager that ever lived, but he is certainly the one with the most longevity.

Another element of the Connie Mack story is his record of being the oldest manager ever to perform the role. When he closed out his final season on October 1, 1950, Mack was eighty-eight years and 221 days old.

JOHN MCGRAW and CASEY STENGEL: Most Pennant Winners

John McGraw and Casey Stengel were very different as human beings, but they were very much alike as managers in their desire to win. Both share a slot at the top of baseball's greatest record for winning the most pennants—ten. And since McGraw managed in the National League with the New York Giants and Stengel was an American League pilot with the New York Yankees, their pennant-winning powers are purely individual accomplishments.

McGraw came from the old Baltimore Orioles to take command of the New York Giants on July 16, 1902. He inherited a last-place team that had had thirteen managers since 1891. The man they called Mugsy immediately released half the players on the roster of the Giants. "With my team," he said, "I'm the czar." Driving the players, innovating, McGraw moved the Giants from a last-place finish in 1902 to a second-place finish in 1903. In his thirty years as manager, the Giants won ten pennants and finished second eleven times.

McGraw's small physical stature contrasted sharply with the giant power that his gait, his face, and his name projected throughout the world of baseball. He was famous for such lines as "The only popularity I know is to win," "Do what I tell you, and I'll take the blame if it goes wrong" and "I do the hiring and the firing around here." For the record, McGraw's Giant pennants came in 1904–05, 1911–13, 1917 and 1921–24.

Casey Stengel was an original. Born on July 30, 1890, in Kansas City, Missouri, he played in the major leagues for fourteen years and managed for twenty-five more, with the Brooklyn Dodgers, the Boston Braves and the New York Yankees, where he hit his stride after all those long years with mediocre teams. "When he arrived on the scene," recalled former Yankee pitcher Eddie Lopat, "we thought we had got us a clown." Casey clowned, but he also managed brilliantly.

Stengel's Yankees won five straight pennants, 1949– 53 (something no other manager has ever been able to duplicate). There were pennants in 1955–58 and another in 1960 for the Yankees of Casey Stengel, bringing his total to ten and making him co-holder with McGraw for the all-time manager's pennant record.

Stengel was known by the nickname the Ole Perfessor, and in a lifetime of doing many things, he had actually held the title of professor. In 1914, he held down the job of coaching spring training baseball at the University of Mississippi and was called Professor Stengel.

In 1969, Stengel was voted the title Baseball's Greatest Manager during the centennial observance of the sport. It was a fitting tribute to the man who had once played under John McGraw and used many of the best techniques of the old Giant pilot and invented others to bring out the best in his teams.

PHENOMENA

Contrived baseball phenomena include: the exploding scoreboard at the Houston Astrodome, the Chicken and his comic cavorting, the sight of 30,000 kids swinging Louisville Slugger bats—gifts from a grateful club management. Fortunately, these pseudo-events have always been kept in perspective as a sideshow of baseball.

This section takes a look at just a few events that were not sideshow material but are part of the historic style and substance of the national pastime.

The Longest Game

At 4:09 A.M. on April 19, 1981, while most of New England slept and the sun slowly crept up the horizon, nineteen glassy-eyed fans filed out of the stands at McCoy Stadium at Pawtucket, Rhode Island. They were the only survivors—witness to thirty-two innings of battle between the Pawtucket Red Sox and the Rochester Red Wings that was suspended in a 2–2 tie by order of International League President Harold Cooper.

Exhausted, groggy, but still "into the game," the players of the PawSox and the Red Wings stumbled out of the little New England ball park knowing they would play again another day. The thirty-two innings lasted eight hours and seven minutes, but Pawtucket manager Joe Morgan wasn't around at the end—he had been ejected from the game in the twenty-first inning.

The marathon contest would have been noteworthy in itself, but coming as it did in the midst of the strike by major league baseball teams, much media attention was drawn to it. On Tuesday, June 23, at 6:00 P.M., 5,756 jammed into McCoy Stadium, a park built in the days of the Franklin Delano Roosevelt WPA endeavors, to watch the second act of the longest game.

"I received more than 171 requests for credentials," said Pawtucket General Manager Mike Tamburro. "Normally no more than seven reporters cover a PawSox game. It had to be the sporting event of the country on that particular day. We had someone from every major daily on the East Coast present. We broadcast to Boston, Baltimore, Rochester and Chicago. We even had a reporter and a photographer who came to cover the event from the *Manachi Daily News* in Tokyo."

Pawtucket's eighth pitcher, Bob Ojeda, took the mound for the top of the thirty-third inning. He yielded a one-out single to Cal Ripken, Jr. Then he struck out Floyd Rayford and got John Valle on a soft fly ball to left field.

Leather-lunged loyalists screamed for Pawtucket to end the marathon as the Red Sox came to bat in the bottom of the thirty-third inning against Steve Grilli, who had been on the Syracuse roster when the first thirty-two innings had been played back in April.

The fifth Rochester pitcher of the epic competition, Grilli's first toss hit Marty Barrett. A single by Chico Walker moved Barrett to third base. An intentional walk to Russ Laribee filled the bases. Cliff Speck relieved Grilli.

Dave Koza came to bat. To that point he had recorded four hits in thirteen at bats. "Having the bases loaded was a dream for me," Koza later recalled. "I think anyone would have liked to be in my shoes." With the count two balls and two strikes, Koza lashed Speck's curveball into left field to score Barrett and give Pawtucket a 3–2 triumph over Rochester and end the longest game in baseball history. "It was justice," said Red Sox manager Joe Morgan. "The guy who played the toughest in the thirty-two innings drives in the winning run."

Grilli's record fell to 0–3 with the loss. "I guess years from now it will be easier to take," he said, "but I felt bad because I let the rest of the guys down. There was a lot of pressure, but I guess I was too pumped up."

The first thirty-two innings of the longest game in baseball history took eight hours and twenty-five minutes to play. The thirty-third inning—the final inning—took just eighteen minutes.

In addition to the record for the most innings ever played and the time, other marks set included most put-outs one team (ninety-nine); most putouts both teams (195); most at bats one team set by Pawtucket (114); most at bats both teams (219); strikeouts one team, Rochester (thirty-four); strikeouts both teams (sixty); assists both teams (eighty-eight); most times at bat, Lee Graham, Dave Koza, Chico Walker (fourteen); most plate appearances, Tom Eaton, Cal Ripken, Dallas Williams (fifteen).

Some of the players who competed in "the longest game" have moved on to perform in the major leagues for the Boston Red Sox and the Baltimore Orioles. And when they meet each other in American League parks, more often than not the conversation gets around to a discussion of the thirty-three innings they played against each other in 1981 at little McCoy Stadium in Pawtucket, Rhode Island.

Major League Baseball's First Night Game

During the Great Depression, financial woes afflicted all enterprises. Baseball was not exempt. The national pastime under the lights proved to be an attraction that helped minor league baseball survive and in some cases prosper. There were instances where night games doubled and tripled minor league attendance.

In 1934, fifteen of the nineteen minor leagues bragged that they had at least one of their parks fitted out with lights for night baseball. One of the most successful of franchises was Columbus in the American Association, aided by night baseball and the promotional skills of Larry MacPhail.

Despite the minor league successes with night games, major league baseball would have nothing to do with it. Most big league executives thought of night games as a passing fancy.

Operating more out of concern that the Cincinnati franchise might go out of business than out of interest in night baseball, National League executives granted permission for the Reds to play seven night games in 1935 provided the seven other National League teams agreed. The 1934 Reds drew only 206,373—less than the team had attracted in eight World Series games with the White Sox in 1919. The club needed something to boost its sagging gate receipts. Larry MacPhail, who had moved up from Columbus to become Cincinnati general manager, promised National League executives that night baseball was the wave of the future.

The first night game in major league history was played at Cincinnati's Crosley Field on May 24, 1935. President Franklin D. Roosevelt, seated in the White House, flicked the remote-control switch that turned on the lights, and 1,090,000 watts of electric power from 632 lamps lit up the field and turned night into day. National League president Ford Frick threw out the first ball. And Cincinnati, behind the six-hit pitching of Paul Derringer, edged the Philadelphia Phillies, 2–1. The spectacle attracted 20,422 fans, about ten times as many as usually came out for a game between the Reds and the Phillies.

Reaction to that first night game was mixed. Some declared that baseball was meant to be played in sunshine and that the lights changed the essential nature of the game. Others thought that the lights would negatively affect the performance of players. Most maintained that night baseball was a way to increase attendance and furnish those who worked all day with the opportunity to see their favorite teams perform at night.

By 1940, there were seventy night games scheduled at major league parks. Only Boston and Chicago in the National League and New York, Boston, Washington and Detroit in the American League were without lights. In 1941, Washington's Griffith Stadium acquired lights. The Boston Braves and New York Yankees put lights in in 1946. A year later the Red Sox erected lights at Fenway. In 1948, Detroit installed lights and every major league team had the capacity to play night baseball.

All-Star Games and World Series competition at night in prime time over national television, and a schedule in some instances dominated by night games—all can be traced back to May 24, 1935, when Larry MacPhail lit up old Crosley Field in major league baseball's first night game.

Greatest Play-Off Game: American League

On October 2, 1978, almost 33,000 crowded into Fenway Park and millions more watched on national television as the New York Yankees opposed the Boston Red Sox in the second one-game play-off in American League history. The scene was straight out of Hollywood.

The teams had finished the 1978 season with identical 99–63 records. Historic rivals, the Yanks and the Sox, like two punchy fighters, had struggled through the 1978 season, only to wind up in this showdown meeting with the entire year boiling down to just one game at Fenway.

Boston was the "hot team," having ended the 1978 campaign with eight straight wins, victors in twelve of their last fifteen games. And they had been able all season to capitalize on their home field edge, winning fifty-nine of eighty-two games played at Fenway. But there were those throughout New England who remembered all the years of the Red Sox–Yankee rivalry, all the years of the Red Sox finishing second behind the New Yorkers. Boston fans lived with bitter memories of victory turned into defeat; they wondered as the play-off game got underway if they would have one more nightmare to add to the collection that woke them in the middle of the night with a vision of a Yankee crossing home plate with a winning, heartbreaking run against the Sox. In 1904, 1938, 1939, 1941, 1942, 1949 and 1977, the Yankees and the Red Sox finished one-two in the American League standings. And in each of those years except 1904 there was a

Yankee pennant. The second-place blues was a factor as Ron Guidry, baseball's best pitcher in 1978, took the mound for the Yanks against Mike Torrez, who just the year before had toiled for New York and who was yearning to defeat them in the play-off.

Sox fans were ecstatic in the second inning when Yastrzemski, the man they affectionately called Captain Carl, rapped a home run down the right field line to give Boston a 1–0 lead. "I thought that when the old man hit the home run that was going to do it," said former Boston broadcaster Hawk Harrelson. "Mike Torrez was throwing the ball real well and he wanted that win bad."

In the sixth inning, Rick Burleson smacked a double and Jerry Remy moved him over to third base with a bunt. A Jim Rice single scored Burleson and Boston had a 2–0 lead, and Sox fans were wild with joy. Fred Lynn smashed a Ron Guidry pitch to deep right field. "I lost the ball for a moment in the sun," said Lou Piniella, "but I recovered and fortunately was able to make the catch." Guidry had been touched up, but was still hanging in as the Yanks came to bat in the top of the seventh down by two runs. Torrez needed just nine more outs and it would be all over. He had allowed just three hits in six innings.

Then the Yanks started their roll. Chris Chambliss singled. Roy White singled. Jim Spencer came up as a pinch hitter for light-hitting Brian Doyle. Spencer was only able to manage to fly out, and Boston breathed a bit less nervously. Bucky Dent was the next scheduled batter.

The Yankee shortstop had batted just .140 during the final twenty games of the 1978 season. A right-handed batter, he had managed just four home runs during the season. Torrez looked in at Dent, who was choking up on his bat, as the two Yankee baserunners took slight leads off the bases.

Dent fouled off the first pitch to him and the ball smacked into his foot, stinging an old injury from battles earlier that frenetic season. Dent moved about attempting to shake off the sting.

In the on-deck circle, Mickey Rivers noticed there was a crack in Dent's bat. Bucky decided to scrap the bat. He stepped back in to face Torrez with a Mickey Rivers bat.

Fenway Park thundered with fans beseeching Torrez to bear down. Charged up, Reggie Jackson screamed at Dent, "Hit the tin, Bucky," pleading for the Yankee short-stop to drive in the two runners on base by slamming the ball off the left field wall.

Around came Torrez' right arm, and the five-foot-nine Dent made contact with the ball, which cleared the infield and gained altitude as it soared in the outfield toward the Green Monster—the left field wall. "The fact that it was at Fenway," recalls Yankee broadcaster Frank Messer, "as soon as it left Bucky's bat, I thought it had a chance. Anytime you hit a fly ball in Boston there's a chance."

On instinct, Carl Yastrzemski scurried back toward the wall. He had been in that position many times as he raced toward the Green Monster. The ball landed over the "tin" and into the left field net.

Fenway Park was silent. Anger and amazement filled the park. Just an instant before, Torrez had been cruising along; now the Yankees were in control. Roy White and Chris Chambliss waited at home plate along with other Yankees and pounded Dent as he scored to give the Bronx Bombers a 3–2 lead.

Lou Piniella remembers the moment: "It was probably the most exciting game I ever played in. We now had the lead on Bucky's home run. We had the Goose ready to short-circuit them. But we knew that Boston was at home and that Boston was going to come back at us."

The Dent home run so unnerved Torrez that he issued a base on balls to Mickey Rivers, who stole second on Bob Stanley, who had come in to replace Torrez. A Munson double to center field gave the Yanks a 4–2 lead as the Sox came to bat in the bottom of the seventh inning.

George Scott's single ended Guidry's stint on the mound. "Goose" Gossage, with a string of thirty appearances in which he had given up no home runs and recorded fifteen saves and six wins, took over. The Sox did not score in the bottom of the seventh.

"I thought it was just an extra run," Reggie Jackson said of his eighth-inning shot that landed deep in the center field bleachers to give the Yankees a 5–2 lead.

Frenzied Boston fans cheered as the game moved to the home half of the eighth inning. When Remy doubled, the ball park rocked. When Yaz singled Remy home, pandemonium prevailed in the stands. Then Carlton Fisk singled. Lynn singled. Yaz scored. The Sox were within a run of tying the score, but Hobson flied out.

Virtually everyone of the more than 33,000 in the stands was on his feet as powerful George Scott faced Gossage. It was strength against strength. Gossage won the battle as he reached back and blew the ball past Scott, striking him out.

The Yankees were retired quickly in the top of the ninth inning, and as the Sox came up for their last licks the noise level at the Fens picked up in intensity. The entire season for the two historic rivals had come down to the last three outs in the bottom of the ninth inning. Many at Fenway had been there before.

Gossage walked Burleson with one out, and Jerry Remy, a contact hitter, stepped in. Remy slashed a sinking liner to right field. The ball dropped in front of Lou Piniella, who trapped it and fired to third base. Burleson, perhaps because of the thundering din of the crowd, perhaps because he was not quite sure if Piniella had caught the ball or not, hesitated and remained at second base. Eddie Yost had been screaming from his third base coach's position for the Sox runner to move up.

With runners now on first and second and one out, Jim Rice came to bat. The Sox outfielder had recorded twenty-eight home runs in 1978 at Fenway. Thousands screamed for him to smash No. 29. Rice ripped a Gossage fastball to deep right field. Piniella caught it and Burleson tagged up and moved on to third base. Second guessers would point out that had Burleson tagged on the previous play, he would have scored.

One out remained for the Sox. Carl Yastrzemski faced Goose Gossage. It was Boston's stylish slugger versus New York's power pitcher.

Remy took his lead off first; Burleson took his lead off third. Munson flashed his signs to Gossage. The signs were ceremonious. "I wasn't going to mess around with breaking junk," Gossage said after the game. "I wasn't going to get beaten by anything but my best. Yastrzemski's the greatest player I've ever played against. I just wound up and threw it as hard as I could. I couldn't tell you where."

The first Gossage fastball was a ball. "If Dent did it,"

a fan's voice was heard over the screaming, "you can do it, Yaz. Hit it out!"

The second Gossage fastball was swung at with full force by Yaz, bidding to hit it out, but all he could muster was a gentle foul fly ball to Nettles, who gloved it near the third base coaching box.

The Yankees won 5–4. For the Sox, the end was bitter. They had managed to come into the play-off on a hot string of eight straight wins only to be denied once again by their historic foes.

Yankee fans were delirious with joy. Red Sox fans were dazed. And what would be known forever as the "damn Bucky Dent pop fly home run into the screen" was one more vision for Sox rooters to add to their nightmare collection of heartbreaking losses to the New York Yankees.

Greatest Play-Off Game: National League

Baseball history abounds in electric moments: incredible pitching performances, dramatic stolen bases, come-from-behind rallies in important games. Of these momentous feats, the home run is in a special category because the electricity is provided with a single swing of the bat. There have been a dozen or so truly dramatic home runs — shots sealing the fate of driving teams. Of all of these, perhaps the most significant one took place during the 1951 baseball season.

It was a time when the Giants played out of the Polo

Grounds in New York and the Dodgers entertained millions in their tiny Brooklyn ball park, Ebbets Field.

The 1951 season began badly for the Giants. Losers of eleven games in a row at one point in the campaign, the Giants were heckled by opponents and written off as "Durocher's grab-bag team." It was a reference to the wholesale switches manager Leo Durocher had effected scuffling about attempting to field the right combination of players he knew he needed to compete with the power-laden Dodgers. "The Lip" traded, sold, shook up his batting order and played athletes at positions that some were unaccustomed to.

Animosity between the Giants of Durocher and the Dodgers of Charlie Dressen was topic A in the sports pages in New York City as the traditional rivals played through the steamy summer days and nights of 1951. In July, Dressen looked down the standings at the struggling Giants and announced to all who would listen: "The Giants is dead." It was the realistic comment of a man who had a lineup that was so powerful that Dressen could afford the luxury of batting Carl Furillo eighth in the order. Furillo batted .295 in 1951.

On August 12, 1951, the Giants trailed the Dodgers by 13½ games in the standings, and the Dressen comment was one even the staunchest supporters of the "Jints" could not easily disagree with. Incredibly, though, from that day to the end of the season the Giants locked into what became known as the "Miracle Run." They won thirty-seven of their final forty-four games—sixteen of them in one frenetic stretch—and closed the gap.

"It was a once-in-a-lifetime situation," recalls Monte Irvin, who batted .312 that year for the Giants and scored a league-leading 121 runs. "How do you catch a team like the Dodgers in a matter of a month and a half? We never said we were going to win it. We said, 'Let's see how close we can get.' We kept on winning. The Dodgers kept on losing. It seemed like we beat everybody in the seventh, eighth and ninth inning."

Durocher's "kind of team" consisted of Irvin, and Willie Mays, brought up in May from Minneapolis, where he had been hitting .477, and Sal Maglie and Larry Jansen, who won twenty-three games each, and Whitey Lockman, who was moved from the outfield to first base, and Bobby Thomson, who was moved from the outfield to third base, and a whole bunch of other scrappy competitors.

The Giants and Dodgers finished the season in a flat-footed tie for first place and met on the first day of October in the first game of the first play-off in the history of the National League. A two-run home run by Bobby Thomson and a Monte Irvin homer paced the 3–1 Giant win. The Dodgers came back in the second game, romping to a 10–0 victory. The split set the stage for the third and final game: October 3, 1951, at the Polo Grounds; twenty-three-game winner Don Newcombe of the Brooklyn Dodgers against twenty-three-game winner Sal Maglie of the New York Giants.

The game began under overcast skies and a threat of rain. Radio play-by-play filtered into schoolrooms, factories, office buildings, city prisons, barbershops. The Wall Street teletype intermingled stock quotations with play-by-play details of the Giant-Dodger battle.

A line single to left in the first inning by Jackie Robinson scored Pee Wee Reese and got the Dodgers off to a 1–0 lead. The score was tied in the bottom of the seventh inning as Monte Irvin doubled and was bunted over to third base by Whitey Lockman and brought home when Bobby Thomson hit a sacrifice fly to deep center field.

Three Dodger runs were scored in the top of the eighth inning, giving them a 4–1 lead. Many of the Dodger fans at the Polo Grounds and the hundreds of thousands listening to the game on the radio thought that the Giants simply could not come back from this three-run deficit.

Durocher and the Giants never gave up. "We knew that Newcombe would make the wrong pitch," said Monte Irvin. "That was his history. In 1950, he made the bad pitch to Dick Sisler that lost the pennant for the Dodgers. Durocher had told us, 'If you stay close to Newk, you can beat him, you can beat him in the last couple of innings.' We had stayed close, but he just blinded us."

The bottom of the eighth inning disheartened even the most fanatical of Giant fans. Don Newcombe, reaching back into his burly frame, struck out the side. However, when he returned to the Dodger dugout, he told Brooklyn manager Charlie Dressen to replace him on the mound for the bottom of the ninth. "I've had it," said Newcombe. "I can't pitch anymore. Take me out of there." Dressen refused.

The Giants came to bat in the bottom of the ninth inning—only three outs left in their miracle season. Alvin Dark, Don Mueller and Monte Irvin were the first three scheduled batters.

A lead-off single by Dark that managed to get through the right side of the infield ignited some hope in Giant fans. Mueller managed to slap the ball past Hodges. The

Giants had runners on first and second and no outs. The Polo Grounds buzzed with noise.

Irvin fouled out to Hodges. Whitey Lockman, a left-handed batter, came up and sliced a two-base hit down the left field line. Dark scored, and Mueller, racing at top speed, slid into third base and broke his ankle. The game was delayed as Mueller was carried from third base across the outfield all the way to the Giant clubhouse in deep center field. Clint Hartung came in as a pinch runner for Mueller.

In the Dodger bullpen, both Carl Erskine and Ralph Branca had warmed up and were ready. Preacher Roe, 22–3, a crafty veteran, was also available, but it was explained later that he had been "saved" to pitch the opening game of the World Series.

With runners on second and third, Ralph Branca relieved Newcombe. Dodger pitching coach Clyde Sukeforth had reported that Branca rather than Erskine should come in to snuff out the Giant rally.

Branca posted a 13–12 record and a 3.26 earned run average during the regular season. "When they brought in Branca," recalls Cal Abrams, a part-time Dodger outfielder in 1951, "I expected something to happen. Ralph was tight and Bobby Thomson was loose. You could tell he was confident. He had hit a couple of homers off Branca that year. He had hit a home run off Branca in the first game of the play-off."

"I didn't know whether they'd pitch to Thomson or not," recalled Leo Durocher. First base was open, and Willie Mays, just a rookie, was on deck. I went up to Thomson and I told him, 'Branca remembers that you hit a slider off him for a home run. He won't throw that today. He'll give you a fastball—right there. Wait for it. Kill it."

Veteran New York Giant announcer Russ Hodges described the moment to millions mesmerized at their radios that October afternoon:

"Bobby Thomson up there swinging. . . . He's had two out of three, a single and a double, and Billy Cox is playing him right on the third base line. . . . One out, last of the ninth. . . . Branca pitches and Bobby takes a strike call on the inside corner. . . ."

From the third base coaching box, Durocher screamed at Thomson: "C'mon, c'mon. He'll throw it again. If you ever hit one, hit one now!"

"Bobby batting at .292." Hodges' voice seemed to grow louder as he filled out the picture. "He's had a single and a double and he drove in the Giants' first run with a long fly to center. Brooklyn leads it, four to two. . . . Hartung down the line at third not taking any chances. . . . Lockman without too big of a lead at second, but he'll be running like the wind if Thomson hits one. . . . Branca throws . . . there's a long drive . . . it's gonna be, I believe . . ." The precise moment was 3:58 P.M., October 3, 1951.

"*. . . the Giants win the pennant!*" Hodges screamed the words at the top of his voice, all semblance of journalistic objectivity gone. *"The Giants win the pennant! The Giants win the pennant!* Bobby Thomson hits into the lower deck of the left field stands . . . *the Giants win the pennant."* Hodges bellowed it out eight times—*"The Giants win the pennant!"*—and then, overcome by the moment and voiceless, he had to yield the microphone.

Pandemonium was on parade at the Polo Grounds.

Bobby Thomson literally pranced about the bases. He would later tell reporters: "When the ball went into the stands, I was more excited than I ever was in my life. It was just the greatest thrill I ever had."

It was not the mightiest of home runs, but it was enough. It went over the left field wall 315 feet from Thomson's point of contact. "When I laid into the pitch," he recalled, "I thought it was gone. But I began to wonder as I broke away from home plate. It started out high and then it began to sink, at least it looked like it was sinking."

Branca prayed for the ball to sink. "I remember turning and looking at Andy Pafko backed against the wall. I knew he couldn't catch the ball. I kept saying, 'Sink, please, sink, sink!'"

The ball did not sink, but went out on a line—triggering the wildest reaction in baseball history to a single home run.

Pafko painfully pushed his body back against the left field wall, straining for the chance to catch the ball. The chance never came. Several Giant players leaped up when Thomson made contact with Branca's pitch and in their rush to see what was happening bumped their heads on the roof of the Giant dugout.

Running out the homer, Thomson leaped into the air as he came around down the third base line and jumped onto home plate and then fell into the arms of his jubilant Giant teammates. Leo Durocher, who later was to say, "In any other ball park in the country the left fielder would have had to come in four or five steps to catch it," was hysterical with delight, with the victory over the Dodgers, with the way it had been accomplished, with the tough, unyielding tenacity of his custom-tailored team.

"Home plate was a mob scene," smiles Thomson. "People were trying to rip pieces off my uniform. I thought I could get killed out there. The fans were out of their minds. I took off for the clubhouse weaving through all those people who were trying to get a piece of me."

Ralph Branca also fought his way through the thousands who had come out on to the playing field at the Polo Grounds. Stunned, saddened by the moment, he was crying, and when he entered the Dodger clubhouse, he leaned against the railing on a staircase and wailed, "Why did it have to happen to me?" Disappointed, angered, some Dodgers kept repeating, "It's over, it's over."

At the exact moment when Bobby Thomson hit what would be known as "the shot heard round the world," thousands of automobile horns blared forth. The noise continued through the streets of New York City for more than ninety minutes. Factory whistles and tugboat horns and garbage-can covers and pots and pans banged at on stoops joined the chorus.

For almost half an hour after the epic home run, there were so many phone calls placed by people in Manhattan and Brooklyn that the New York Telephone Company reported that it was almost unable to accommodate the load.

The frenzied celebration by hysterical Giant fans went on for hours after the game had ended. Fans screamed and hugged each other; they danced about in center field and leaped for joy. Hundreds milled about the steps leading to the clubhouse in center field clamoring for Bobby Thomson to come out for a bow. When the man they called "the Staten Island Scot" appeared on the steps, he took a little bow as rabid, ecstatic fans cheered and applauded him.

The Bobby Thomson home run would forevermore be known as "the Miracle at Coogan's Bluff." Many more people than filled the ball park would tell their friends that they were there in person. Ralph Branca would become a recluse for a while. The fans of the Brooklyn Dodgers would second-guess Charlie Dressen for years. Willie Mays, the on-deck batter, would tell the same story about how he was so relieved that he did not have to come to bat with all that pressure on him.

And Bobby Thomson, a handsome, quiet, unassuming man, would tell and retell the "shot heard round the world" thousands of times: what it felt like, what kind of pitch he hit, how he was to be remembered for the home run.

Because it was New York Giants versus the Brooklyn Dodgers, two teams that are no more, because it was the last pitch of the last inning of the last game of the second play-off in National League history, because it capped one of the most remarkable comebacks in all of baseball history—the Giants coming back from a 13½-game deficit against one of the most powerful Brooklyn Dodger teams ever—these things made the Miracle at Coogan's Bluff especially memorable. Thomson would play out his fifteen-year major league career and record 264 home runs, but the magic one he managed on that October 3, 1951, is the one he and millions would never forget.

JOE NUXHALL:
The Youngest Player

During the World War II years, most major league baseball teams were an odd assortment of over-the-hill athletes and not-quite-ready-for-prime-time performers. Symbolic of these was Joe Nuxhall, a fifteen-year-old on the roster of the Cincinnati Reds, who attended high school during the week and showed up for night and weekend games.

One sunny June afternoon, the Reds were being destroyed 13–0 by the St. Louis Cardinals and Cincinnati manager Bill McKechnie summoned Nuxhall in to pitch. When the right-hander took the mound in the ninth inning, he was exactly fifteen years, ten months and eleven days old—the youngest player ever to see action in a major league game.

Nuxhall walked the first batter he faced and then was able to retire the next two. Then he walked four batters in a row, uncorked a wild pitch, and gave up two singles. When McKechnie mercifully took Nuxhall out of the game, five runs had been charged to him and his earned run average for the two-thirds of an inning was 67.50.

That June 10, 1944, is something Nuxhall will never forget. "Players were scarce because of the war. Bill McKechnie decided it was a good time to put me in a ball game. I guess a lot of the fans thought they'd never see that kid again."

They did. At the age of twenty-three, Nuxhall came

up from the minors and pitched big league baseball for fifteen seasons, recording 135 wins.

SATCHEL PAIGE:
The Oldest Player

One of the most colorful players who ever performed in the major leagues, and definitely the oldest, Satchel Paige was a rookie with the Cleveland Indians in 1948. He refused to say how old he was. Estimates placed him at the time at somewhere between forty-two and forty-nine. Paige would tell reporters he was "anywhere between thirty and seventy."

The long, lean Paige won six of seven decisions for the 1948 Indians and recorded a 2.47 earned run average. The next year he won four games and lost seven. A member of the St. Louis Browns in 1951, Paige won twelve games, striking out nearly 100 batters. He was selected to the American League All-Star team. Though his fastball was gone and his famed "hesitation pitch" (pausing in mid-windup) was declared illegal in the majors, pitching with his head, Paige was one of the top relief hurlers of 1951. He saw limited action in 1952–53, performed for three innings for the 1965 Kansas City Athletics, and then was done as an active performer.

Mythic, legendary Leroy Satchel Paige was born in Mobile, Alabama, according to the best available evi-

dence, not before 1899 and not later than 1906. His youth
was spent running about with gangs of boys. There was
a stint in a reformatory where he allegedly learned how
to throw a baseball.

Part showman, all athlete, at six feet three and 150
pounds or so, with overly long arms, Paige proved to be
a pitching machine. Banned for many years from playing
in the major leagues because of the color barrier, the
reedy-voiced Paige pitched with a variety of teams all
over the world season after season. It is estimated that
he hurled in more than 2,500 games, averaging in his
prime about five appearances a week.

JACKIE ROBINSON:
The First Black Player

Brooklyn was bathed in brilliant sunshine on April 15,
1947, but spring's tempting promise did not last. By
afternoon, the day turned raw. Workers assigned to build
the Brooklyn Battery Tunnel were on strike; diplomats
at the United Nations held a lengthy discussion seeking
to firm up plans for the establishment of an organization
to control atomic energy.

At Ebbets Field in Brooklyn, the Dodgers opposed
Boston in the baseball season opener for both teams.
Many of the 26,623 fans who came to the little ball park
wore fashionable new spring clothes. Many were not even
baseball fans. Many wore "I'm For Jackie" buttons, badges

signifying their approval of the historic debut of the first black man to play major league baseball.

Just four days before, Brooklyn Dodgers general manager Branch Rickey had announced the purchase of the contract of Jackie Robinson from the Montreal Royals (the top farm team of the Dodgers). And Robinson, a grandson of slaves, a former four-star athlete at UCLA, informed that he would open the season at first base for the Dodgers said: "I'm thrilled. It's just what I've been waiting for. I'm just going to take a cut at the ball every time a good one comes over the plate, try to connect, run as fast as I can and play the game hard and clean."

A solitary black man on the playing field, his blue No. 42 on the back of his white Brooklyn Dodgers home uniform, the muscular Robinson took his position at first base that April 15.

Some of the fans sat in the outfield box seats that had been constructed by advancing the left field and left center field stands fourteen feet. Some of the fans were on their feet most of the time, squealing and screaming each time the twenty-eight-year-old Robinson touched the ball or came to bat.

Brooklyn-born sportscaster Stan Lomax recalls the day: "I was there and the general feeling was that we've got a keg of dynamite here—is anybody going to touch off the fuse?"

The rookie Robinson, batting against Boston's crafty Johnny Sain, slammed the ball to shortstop in his first turn at bat. It should have been a routine out. Nothing with Robinson was ever routine. The ball and Robinson arrived at first base at about the same time. Umpire Al Barlick called Robinson out. Angered, Robinson stepped toward the umpire prepared to protest. Then he retreated, under control, and returned to the Dodger dugout. Branch Rickey had prepared him well. Argument, Rickey had told him, could win a battle, but restraint would win the war that Robinson had to wage as baseball's first black player.

In his second plate appearance, Robinson flied out to left field. In his final at bat of the game he grounded into a rally-killing double play. The statistical debut of Jackie Roosevelt Robinson was a muted one. He batted three times and did not record a hit. He had eleven putouts at first base. He did not make an error in the field. The Dodgers won the game 5–3, and the first of Robinson's 1,382 major league games was now a matter of record.

Robinson, through those first few seasons, endured assassination threats, racial epithets, tags by opponents that were more like gloved punches, threatened strikes, loneliness and segregation. He endured all of this and ultimately prevailed. Brooklyn lined up solidly behind the man it called Robby. And his face, his voice, his walk, his stance, his style became synonymous with the Dodger brand of baseball. He led the Dodgers to pennants in 1947, 1949, 1952, 1953, 1955, and 1956, and broke ground for a pipeline of black talent that has contributed its verve and skill to enrich the national pastime. He led the National League in batting in 1949 with a .342 average. Twenty times in his career he stole home. Playing under the most intense pressures, he recorded a .311 lifetime batting average.

Today Jackie Robinson stands out as a member of baseball's Hall of Fame, one of the most famous athletes ever produced in the United States, one of the greatest competitors in the history of baseball. Yet, at the start, on April 15, 1947, he was the underdog, a black man playing a white man's game.

The Final Tripleheader

The first and almost certainly last tripleheader in the twentieth century was played at Pittsburgh during the final week of the 1920 season. The marathon contest was motivated by Pirate owner Barney Dreyfuss, whose team with two days' play remaining in the season was in fourth place, 3½ games behind the third-place-defending World Champion Cincinnati Reds. A sweep of the Reds and their loss in a season finale and a Pirate win would give the Pirates third place and a share in World Series receipts. Despite the protestations of the Cincinnati ownership, Dreyfuss received permission from league president John A. Heydler to play the tripleheader against the Reds.

Game one began at noon. Pirate manager George Gibson started twenty-four-game winner Wilbur Cooper and supported him with a team that included the skilled outfielder Max Carey, first baseman Charlie Grimm, and two rookies, third baseman Clyde Barnhart and shortstop Pie Traynor. Cincinnati fielded its set lineup that had played together for the past two seasons: Jake Daubert (1B), Morrie Rath (2B), Heinie Groh (3B), Larry Kopf (SS), Edd Roush (CF), Pat Duncan (LF) and "Greasy" Neale (RF). Bill Rairden, a reserve catcher, was behind the plate for Ray Fisher, who was winding up a journeyman pitching career.

The Reds hammered out ten hits and eight runs off Cooper in 2⅔ innings and romped to a 13–4 win. The victory clinched third place for Cincinnati, but the Dreyfuss plan to play the advertised tripleheader still held. The first game had taken only two hours and three minutes to play. A footnote to baseball history was the two errors Pie Traynor made in this game at shortstop, and the general feeling that emerged that he would one day be more valuable at third base.

A seven-run seventh inning gave the Reds a 7–3 win in the second game despite the fact that most of the Pirate regulars played (with the exception of Traynor) and most of the Cincinnati starters rested. Four pitchers performed for the Reds in that second game: Rube Bressler played right field; Dutch Ruethler was at first; center field was manned by Fritz Coumbe, and Buck Benton was the only hurler in his regular position—he pitched. A fifth pitcher got into the act when Cincinnati's best hurler, Hod Eller, came into the game as an infield sub and recorded three hits.

Game three began with a switch: Cincinnati was given the opportunity to be the home team despite the fact that the game was played in Pittsburgh. The game was called after six innings because of darkness. Pittsburgh salvaged a 6–0 win behind the four-hit pitching of Jughandle Johnny Morrison in the only start of his rookie season.

On the final Sunday of the season, a day after the tripleheader, the Reds lost their game to St. Louis while Pittsburgh was victorious in Chicago. The Reds, however, had clinched third place and their World Series share of $10,744.14, which was divided up among some two dozen or so athletes. It hardly seemed worth playing a tripleheader just for that.

Most Losses by a Club in One Season

In 1960, Casey Stengel managed the New York Yankees to a first-place finish. The team won ninety-seven games and lost just fifty-seven for a .630 percentage. By 1962, his world turned upside down. He was the manager of the New York Mets in their first season of existence.

A bumbling collection of castoffs, not-quite-ready for prime-time baseball players, paycheck collectors, callow youth—the Mets were highly skilled in underwhelming the opposition.

The team finished tenth in a ten-team league. They finished 60½ games out of first place. They lost 120 games, the most in baseball history, and won forty. "When I go back in my mind and look at that season," said Stengel, "I wonder how we ever won forty."

The New York Mets of 1962 were capably equipped to break the all-time losing record of 117 set by Connie Mack's 1916 Philadelphia Athletics. Richie Ashburn, one of the only solid performers for the Mets that season (he batted .306), recalled: "It was the only time I went to a ball park in the major leagues and nobody expected you to win."

The 1962 season began badly for the Mets and got worse. They lost their first ten games. "The trouble is,"

Stengel said, "we are in a losing streak at the wrong time. If we were losing like this in the middle of the season, nobody would notice. But we are losing at the beginning of the season, and this sets up the possibility of losing all 162 games."

Some of the "outstanding" performers on the '62 Mets who played in the odd environs of the Polo Grounds, the former home of the New York Giants, included Jay Hook, who could talk for hours about why a curveball curved (he had a master's degree in engineering) but could not throw one consistently; "Choo-Choo" Coleman, an excellent lowball catcher, but the team had very few lowball pitchers; and "Marvelous Marv" Throneberry, a Mickey Mantle look-alike in the batter's box, but that's where the resemblance ended.

Spoiled with the likes of Mantle, Yogi Berra, Roger Maris, and Whitey Ford, day after day Stengel would suffer through the saga of the bumbling Mets. In desperation—some say it was the day he saw pitcher Al Jackson go fifteen innings, yield but three hits, and lose the game on two errors committed by Marvelous Marv— Casey bellowed out his plaintive query: "Can't anybody here play this game?"

The record clearly shows not too many could. In addition to losing more games in one season than any team in history, the Mets managed to bungle their way into other all-time negative stat categories. Their staff yielded the most home runs in a season (192) and the most wild pitches (seventy-one) and had the first two twenty-game losers (Al Jackson and Roger Craig) since the 1936 Philadelphia Phillies.

The 1962 Met pitching staff had the worst earned run

average, gave up the most runs and hits, and hit the most batters of any team in the National League. Booting, swatting, dropping baseballs, the team's fielding average was .967, lowest in the league. The Mets averaged more than an error a game and wound up with 210 miscues for the season—also tops in the league. Roger Craig's 4.51 earned run average was the best of all Met pitchers. He lost twenty-four games, most in the league.

Some solace could be taken in the fact that the Mets were able to draw 922,530—the best home attendance by a last-place club in history. And more solace could be taken from the fact that three other teams finished more games out of first place than did the 1962 Mets. The Cleveland Spiders in 1899 were eighty games off the pace; the 1906 Boston National League club was 66½ games out; and the 1939 St. Louis Browns finished last, 64½ games out of first place.

When Stengel was informed about all the negative records compiled by the 1962 Mets he thought a moment and then used a phrase he had uttered many times to characterize his successes as a Yankee manager: "You know, we coulda never done it without the players."

Most Wins by a Club in One Season

The 1909 Pittsburgh Pirates won 110 games, as did the 1927 New York Yankees. The 1954 Cleveland Indians won 111 games. But the all-time record by a team for wins in a single season, 116, is held by the 1906 Chicago

Cubs, and it's going to take some doing for any club to top that mark.

Anchored by an awesome pitching staff and buttressed by skillful fielding, the 1906 Cubs blended all aspects of baseball. On the road, the team was superb, winning sixty of seventy-five games played. In tight ball games, the Cubs excelled, winning nine 1–0 contests. They took over first place in the National League on May 28 and remained there for the rest of the season. In August, the Cubs won twenty-six of twenty-nine games played. They wound up the year with a 116–36 record and a .763 percentage—twenty games ahead of the second-place New York Giants.

It was a team that dominated most statistical categories. First in the league in runs (704), batting average (.262), hits (1,316), triples (seventy-one), slugging average (.339), fielding average (.969), strikeouts by its pitching staff (702), shutouts (twenty-eight), and earned run average (1.76), the Cubs also finished second in stolen bases (283), just five behind the Giants.

The heart of the team was its three twenty-game winners: Three-Finger Brown, left-hander Jack Pfiester and Big Ed Reulbach. The three hurlers combined for a record of 66–18. Brown's earned run average was a microscopic 1.04, and he led the league in shutouts with nine. Pfiester (who lost eight games for the most defeats on the Cub staff) was known as Jack the Giant Killer because of his winning ways against John McGraw's Giants. His 1.56 earned run average was second best in the league. Reulbach posted a 1.65 earned run average, lost just four games, recorded a winning percentage of .833, and had a string of a dozen straight wins. Brown, Pfiester, and

Reulbach were a potent trio, but the staff of the Cubs still had more able arms to back them up.

There was Carl Lundgren (17–6) and two midseason acquisitions who boasted identical 12–3 records, Orvall Overall and Jack Taylor. The six top Cub pitchers combined for a winning percentage of better than .700.

Supporting this pitching staff was an infield that consisted of player-manager Frank Chance at first base, the famed double-play combination of Joe Tinker and Johnny Evers, and the talented Harry Steinfeldt at third base, who led the league in fielding percentage at his position and batted .327, second only to National League batting champion Honus Wagner. Chance was first in stolen bases in the senior circuit and batted .319. He led by example.

Catcher Johnny Kling was a .312 hitter who recorded 520 putouts (best in the league) and paced all catchers with a .982 fielding average. He kept opposition baserunners alert with his powerful arm and willingness to throw at any time. Pat Moran was his able backup.

The Cub outfield was very strong defensively, with Jimmy Scheckard in left field, Jimmy Slagle in center and Frank Schulte in right field. Of the three, "Wildfire" Schulte was the best hitter. He batted .281 and was the league leader in triples.

"The Chicago team far outclassed any of its competitors," said the *Reach Official Guide* for 1907, "in every department of play." They were "the best balanced team in the world... with the best pitching corps of any club, two of the best catchers in the profession, a fast-fielding and hard-hitting infield and outfield, more than the average number of quick thinkers and fast runners." It was a fairly accurate description, and although the Cubs lost in the World Series to their crosstown rivals, the White Sox, their 116 wins in a season is the Mount Everest of club records.

Highest World Series Share

The seventy-ninth World Series produced record winners' shares of $43,279.69 for thirty-two members of the St. Louis Cardinals, the split given to those who were voted full shares. The '82 Series between the Redbirds and the Milwaukee Brewers produced a record player pool of $4,500,467.78 and eclipsed the mark set in 1981 by the New York Yankees and the Los Angeles Dodgers.

Just how far baseball has come since the first World Series played in 1903 is reflected in that year's winners' share of $1,182. The 1982 St. Louis winners' share was almost $10,000 a player more than that of 1980 World Series victors.

ENDURANCE

Steve Garvey talks about playing for six more seasons without missing a game and breaking Lou Gehrig's record for consecutive games played in. Jim Kaat indicates that he will take it one season at a time in an attempt to add to his record as having pitched more years in the major leagues than any other hurler in baseball history. Pete Rose has at his fingertips all the statistics of his career and all the marks set by others that he hopes to shatter— if he stays healthy and keeps on playing.

Strength, stamina and pride are the bricks that form the foundation for all those who have set and are setting and will set baseball's greatest records of endurance. This section takes a close-up look at "staying power" accomplishments.

LOU GEHRIG:
2,130 Consecutive Games Played

On June 2, 1925, Yankee veteran Wally Pipp was hit on the side of the head during batting practice. "Take a rest today," manager Miller Huggins told the Yankee veteran, who was downing aspirin tablets in the locker room. "I'm going to start young Gehrig in your place." Huggins then told the six-foot, 200-pound first baseman that he was starting the game and that if he did well he would become a regular on the Yankees. Gehrig rapped out a double and two singles in the game.

The misconception is that when Gehrig replaced Pipp, the fabled streak of 2,130 games started. It actually began the day before when Gehrig was called on as a pinch hitter for Pee Wee Wanninger, the player who, ironically, replaced Everett Scott. A shortstop, Scott had the record for consecutive games played, 1,307, until he was replaced by Wanninger.

Signed out of Columbia University, Gehrig played for two seasons in Hartford in the Eastern League and came up to the New York Yankees in 1923 and played in thirteen games, then in ten games in 1924. From that moment on June 1, when he pinch-hit for Wanninger, for the next fourteen years, the Iron Horse never missed being in the Yankee lineup.

He played when it mattered a great deal and when it didn't matter at all. He played with pain and with pride. He drove himself and his Yankee teammates season after season, a steadying, solid force.

A left-handed batter and thrower, Gehrig recorded 493 home runs, ten World Series homers and a .340 lifetime batting average. Three times he was named the American League's Most Valuable Player. Five times he led the league in RBIs. Three times he was the American League home run king.

Twice during the streak, Gehrig was beaned. Once he was hit by pitcher Earl Whitehill and another time by Ray White of Norfolk, Virginia, in an exhibition game. There were those who thought he had a fractured skull and that the streak was over, but the man they called Iron Horse played the next day and banged out three triples.

On July 13, 1934, pain in his back from what was diagnosed as lumbago was so severe that he had to be helped off the field in the first inning in a game against the Detroit Tigers. The streak stood at 1,426. Gehrig was in such pain that it seemed there was no way he could manage to play the next day. He did play, after a fashion. Listed first in the Yankee batting order and tabbed to play shortstop, he singled to lead off the game and was removed for a pinch runner.

It was said that "nothing short of a locomotive will stop Lou Gehrig. He will go on forever." Near the final third of the 1938 season, the Iron Horse began to falter.

What had troubled him off and on during his career and was diagnosed as lumbago was actually a destructive disease caused by a deadly virus. As the 1938 season ended, no one knew what was really wrong with Lou Gehrig, but it was clear that his great strength was waning. His hand would tremble as he held a cup of coffee, and he would sometimes lose his grip and drop the cup. His zestful, energetic performance on the playing field had become dulled, muted, lethargic.

In spring training in 1939, the disease grew stronger. Gehrig grew weaker. His Yankee teammates and his wife, Eleanor, told him to rest, to not drive himself. They argued that the record was safe and that no one would ever come along and break it.

The Pride of the Yankees pushed himself, with disastrous results.

The season of 1939 began, and Lou Gehrig once again was positioned at first base for the New York Yankees. He would take that famous big swing, but he would only pop up; little fly balls replaced the booming gargantuan home runs that he had hit in the past. Still he played on. Once at Yankee Stadium he bent over to tie his shoelaces and fell down. He would trip over his own feet. Manager Joe McCarthy would look away. He filled Gehrig's name in on the lineup card day after day. McCarthy just could not break the heart of the man who had meant so much to the Yankees by taking him out of the lineup.

Gehrig would come home to his wife shaken, suffering. "Stop playing, Lou," she pleaded. "Take some time off and get yourself checked out and find out what is wrong with you."

"I have to play on," Gehrig pleaded, and there were tears in the big man's eyes. "I will be able to work it out. This is the only way for me to go."

On April 30, 1939, Lou Gehrig decided there was another way to go. After a game in which he had gone 0–4, he sought out manager Joe McCarthy in the hotel lobby. "You'd better take me out, Joe," Gehrig said. "I guess that's all." It was the last game he ever played.

Yankee pitcher Lefty Gomez attempted to soften the moment. "Hey, Lou," he cracked. "It took fifteen years to get you out of the game. Sometimes I'm out of there in fifteen minutes."

On May 2, 1939, in one of baseball's somber ironies, Wally Pipp, whose place Gehrig had taken those 2,130 games away, came down from his home in Grand Rapids, Michigan, to watch the Yankee-Tiger game and Lou Gehrig perform. Instead he saw the Iron Horse standing alone at home plate giving out the lineup card with his name left off it. At age thirty-six, the highest-paid player in baseball, Gehrig, although he probably didn't know it at that moment, was engaging in his last hurrah as an active player.

An announcement was made to the fans about Gehrig's voluntary withdrawal from the starting lineup. As the Yankee stalwart slowly walked back to the dugout, he was given a huge ovation by the crowd at the Tiger ballpark. Taking off his cap, Gehrig doffed it to the fans, then settled into a corner of the Yankee bench all by himself. One can only wonder what thoughts he had.

When Babe Dahlgren, Gehrig's replacement, who had waited three years for his chance, homered in the third inning, the first person out of the Yankee dugout to congratulate him was the man they once called Columbia Lou.

Shock waves reverberated throughout the world of baseball at the news of Gehrig's streak coming to an end. "Lou just told me he felt it would be best for the club if I took him out of the lineup," said McCarthy. "I asked him if he really felt that way. He told me he was serious. He feels blue. He is dejected. I told him it would be as he wished. Like everybody else, I'm sorry to see it happen. I told him not to worry. Maybe the warm weather will bring him around. He's been a great ball player. Fellows like him come along once in a hundred years. More than that, he's been a vital part of the Yankee club since he started. He's always been a perfect gentleman, a credit to baseball. We'll miss him. You can't escape that fact. But I think he's doing the proper thing."

"I decided last Sunday night on this move," Gehrig told reporters after the game, the first Yankee game in fifteen years that he had not played in. "I haven't been a bit of good to the team since the season started." When he benched himself, Gehrig was batting .143—almost 200 points below his lifetime batting average.

"It would not be fair to the boys," Gehrig continued, "to Joe, or to the baseball public for me to try going on. In fact, it wouldn't be fair to myself, and I'm the last consideration. It's tough to see your mates on base, have a chance to win a ball game, and not be able to do anything about it. McCarthy has been swell about it all the time. He'd let me go until the cows came home. He is that considerate of my feelings, but I knew in Sunday's game"—Gehrig's last, on April 30, 1939, a Yankee loss to the Washington Senators—"that I should get out of there. I went up there four times with men on base. Once there were two there. A hit would have won the ball game for the Yankees, but I missed leaving five grounded as the Yankees lost. Maybe a rest will do me some good. Maybe it won't. Who knows? Who can tell? I'm just hoping."

On June 19, 1939, on his thirty-sixth birthday, Lou Gehrig left the Mayo Clinic with a sealed envelope. The results of his diagnosis and examinations were in it: "Mr. Gehrig is suffering from amyotrophic lateral sclerosis. This type of illness involves the motor pathways and cells of the central nervous system and in lay terms is known as a form of chronic poliomyelitis (infantile paralysis). The nature of this trouble makes it such that Mr. Gehrig will be unable to continue his active participation as a baseball player."

Gehrig returned to the Yankees and tarried for a while like a great bowed oak. Still the captain, still the Pride of the Yankees, he brought the lineup card out to the umpires before each game and watched other men play baseball from his corner seat in the Yankee dugout. On July 5, 1939, he called it a career. The Yankees won the World Series that year and voted the Iron Horse a share of the proceeds. In December of 1939, Lou Gehrig was inducted into the Baseball Hall of Fame. On June 2, 1941—exactly sixteen years to the day after he replaced Wally Pipp as the New York Yankee first baseman— Gehrig died, seventeen days short of his thirty-eighth birthday.

YOGI BERRA:
Mr. World Series

Lawrence Peter Berra, better known as Yogi, was a top star for the New York Yankees from 1946 to 1965. He is remembered for his baseball talent as well as for some of his more colorful expressions.

Through his long seasons as a crafty catcher and clutch hitter, Berra saw all kinds of baseball games. "It's not over till it's over" was one of his classic lines to describe how anything could happen in the national pastime and the game of life.

When he first joined the Bronx Bombers, a few not so kind teammates made some disparaging remarks about the way Berra's face was put together. "You don't hit with your face" was Yogi's reply. "A face has nothing to do with winning."

Berra was an expert in both winning and hitting. Inducted into the Hall of Fame in 1971, Berra's regular-season accomplishments and especially post-season records made him a worthy inductee.

Yogi played in more World Series (fourteen) and more World Series games (seventy-five) and had more World Series at bats (259), hits (seventy-one), and doubles (ten) than any other player in history. As a catcher, he cut down thirty-six base-stealing attempts in World Series play for another record.

Reggie Jackson has been dubbed Mr. October, but it is Yogi who should be called Mr. World Series. The Fall Classic's history is filled with examples of Berra at his best.

He was the man behind the plate calling the pitches as Don Larsen hurled the only perfect game in World Series history in game five of the 1956 World Series against the Brooklyn Dodgers. It was Yogi in game three of the 1947 World Series who recorded the first pinch-hit homer in the post-season Classic. His two-run homer in the fourth and final game of the 1950 Series triggered the Yankee 5–2 victory over the Philadelphia Phillies. In 1956, in game two, Berra blasted the fifth grand slam home run in World Series history and then came back in game seven to lash two more home runs, capping a 9–0 Yankee rout of the Dodgers and a World Series championship.

He tied with Mickey Mantle (they both hit at least one home run in nine World Series). Other Series records held by Berra include driving in at least one run in eleven Series, scoring at least one run in twelve Series and walking at least one time in thirteen Series. Perhaps his World Series record of records is that he played for ten World Championship teams—and with free agentry and expansion it seems doubtful that any other player will ever come close to that record.

PETE ROSE:
The Record Man

In 1982, Pete Rose completed his twentieth major league season and needed just 322 hits to tie Ty Cobb's all-time record of 4,191. He broke Stan Musial's National League record for hits in 1981. Born the year of Joe DiMaggio's fifty-six-game hitting streak, Rose shares with Wee Willie Keeler the National League record for hitting safely in forty-four straight games.

A durable, dedicated performer, the switch-hitting Rose once was referred to as Charlie Hustle because of his all-out style of play. By the time his career is concluded, he'll probably be known as the Record Man. He already has quite a few lines in the record book.

Rose played in every one of the Phillies games in the 1982 season and passed Willie Mays, Stan Musial and Ty Cobb on the all-time list. Going into the 1983 season, only Carl Yastrzemski (3,189) and Hank Aaron (3,298) had played in more games in their careers than Rose, whose mark stood at 3,099. The 1982 season also saw Rose play in his 626th straight game.

The scrappy Philadelphia first baseman ranks sixth in all-time total bases, fifth in runs scored, fourth in doubles, and second in singles. He has more seasons (ten) with 200 hits than any other player in history. He is the all-time leader in major league at bats.

Driven to excel, determined to break every record he can, Rose has done a great deal of thinking about modern-day player performance as contrasted with the stars of yesterday. "The hitters in the other eras were not better than the ones playing today," he says. "If Ty Cobb came up today he wouldn't be hitting .400. The game has changed. The outfielders are faster. Night baseball makes a big difference. And the pressure is greater today when you have to please 20,000,000 watching on TV, not just the 20,000 in the old days who watched the games at the park."

The first singles hitter to earn $100,000, Rose has more five-hit games (eight) than any other players except Max Carey (nine) and Ty Cobb (fourteen). On August 5, 1979, he went into the record books again, becoming the all-time best singles hitter in National League history by breaking Honus Wagner's mark at Pittsburgh with single number 2,427.

With all the hitting records possessed by Rose and within reach of the fiery competitor, not too much attention has been focused on his fielding accomplishments. He has excelled there, too. Rose holds the major league record for the highest fielding percentage lifetime by an outfielder (1,000 or more games), .992. In 1980, he compiled the best fielding percentage of any first baseman, .997, with just five errors in 1,555 total chances. In 1981, Rose set another major league record by starting at his fifth different position in the All-Star Game (2B-LF-RF-3B-1B).

The 1962 Rookie of the Year, the 1973 National League Most Valuable Player, the 1975 World Series Most Valuable Player, the National League Player of the Decade

(1970s) named by the *Sporting News* and *Baseball Magazine,* and the Athlete of the Decade (1970s) named by the American Cancer Society, Pete Rose is the record man of record men. Each time he swings the bat, throws or catches a ball, or drives in or scores a run, he adds to his milestone accomplishments.

HARVEY FROMMER is an associate professor of writing and speech at New York City Technical College in the City University of New York. A well-known sports author and lecturer, he has written fourteen books, five of them dealing with baseball.